The Treasures of Darkness

The Treasures of Darkness

Edwin L. Carpenter

XULON PRESS

Xulon Press
2301 Lucien Way #415
Maitland, FL 32751
407.339.4217
www.xulonpress.com

© 2019 by Edwin L. Carpenter

All rights reserved solely by the author. The author guarantees all contents are original and do not infringe upon the legal rights of any other person or work. No part of this book may be reproduced in any form without the permission of the author. The views expressed in this book are not necessarily those of the publisher.

Scripture quotations taken from the King James Version (KJV) – *public domain.*

Scripture quotations taken from the Holy Bible, New International Version (NIV). Copyright © 1973, 1978, 1984, 2011 by Biblica, Inc.™. Used by permission. All rights reserved.

Printed in the United States of America.

ISBN-13: 9781545679708

THE TREASURES OF DARKNESS

Edwin L. Carpenter

XULON PRESS

Xulon Press
2301 Lucien Way #415
Maitland, FL 32751
407.339.4217
www.xulonpress.com

© 2019 by Edwin L. Carpenter

All rights reserved solely by the author. The author guarantees all contents are original and do not infringe upon the legal rights of any other person or work. No part of this book may be reproduced in any form without the permission of the author. The views expressed in this book are not necessarily those of the publisher.

Scripture quotations taken from the King James Version (KJV) – *public domain*.

Scripture quotations taken from the Holy Bible, New International Version (NIV). Copyright © 1973, 1978, 1984, 2011 by Biblica, Inc.™. Used by permission. All rights reserved.

Printed in the United States of America.

ISBN-13: 9781545679708

The Treasures of Darkness

———◆———

This book is lovingly dedicated to my wonderful wife Jackie, to my beloved son Daniel and his wife Kristen, to my twin brother Bill and my brother-in-law Bill Cipponeri for their encouragement, and to the memory of my grandparents, Henry and Emma Fornash.

Table of Contents

Acknowledgements v
The Treasures of Darkness by Edwin L. Carpenter 1
Treasures 6
Holmes and Watson and a Funny Moment 8
A Smile Can Make a Big Difference 10
Love is All-Powerful 11
God Does Not Hold Back Good Things 12
New York City, Wow! 14
The Empty Nest 17
It's New! 19
A Spunky Daughter-in-Law 21
Climbing out of Holes 23
Jingle Bells at a Funeral?! 25
Laughter Helps 27
Call 9-1-1 29
Placed Here for a Reason 32
Changing Seasons 35
Mentors 38
Journey's End 41
A Nice Conclusion 46

The Hardship of Ministry 49
Blood is Thicker than Water 51
Meeting some Neat People 53
Burdens and Buried Treasure 55
Pray About Everything! 57
Temporary Obstacles. 59
The Fonz is Grateful 61
Following Moses. 62
God Never Runs Out of Blessings!. 64
The Waiting Game 65
Silence. 67
Our Weakness and God's Strength 69
The Journal 71
The Celebration of Life! 73
Frustrations but Renewals. 76
 Unusual Answers 78
Sympathy for Others on Their Bad Days 80
Jobs: The Good, the Bad, and the Ugly 82
Reunion: A Wonderful Word. 84
In a Jam but don't fear: Jesus will show up!. 86
Encouragement in the Darkness 88
The Treasures of Darkness: Adversity 90
There's Hope for this Life! 92
Timing is Everything. 94
Sincerity Meets Sarcasm but Keep Knocking on the Door. 96
Face the Music 98
Spend Your Time Wisely 102
Faith Sees the Invisible. 103
God has Our Number 105
God Rises 107

Treasures Lie Below 109
Sad to Glad 110
Imitation 111
A Thousand Faces 113
Time Brings Change 115
Dreams Can Come True 117
Good Intentions. 119
Second Chances 120
Now would be Good, Lord! 123
 Common Sense 125
That Hurts! 128
Forgetfulness can be Good 131
Perseverance Pays. 132
Humility Helps 134
Common Ground 136
Attitude, Attitude! 137
Determined Devin. 139
Is there a Song in Your Heart? 141
Believe in the Darkness 143
Coincidence or Christ? 145
Praying in the Shower. 148
It Worked Out Just Fine 150
Keep Praying! God uses Unlikely People. 151
Mercy 152
Running on Empty? 154
Be Encouraged! God is Faithful! 156
Noble Goals 157
Temper! Temper! Temper! 158
Seed Planter 160
Keep Moving Forward 162

More than One Way to Receive an Answer to Prayer.........164
Confess the Ugly....................................166
Your Gift 168
Eyes on the Only Perfect Man to Ever Live.............. 170
Slow but Worth the Wait............................. 172
God Uses Imperfect People 173
Faith with Works is Active Faith......................175
Evidence 177
The Summary 179

Treasures Lie Below 109
Sad to Glad 110
Imitation 111
A Thousand Faces 113
Time Brings Change 115
Dreams Can Come True 117
Good Intentions. 119
Second Chances 120
Now would be Good, Lord! 123
 Common Sense 125
That Hurts! 128
Forgetfulness can be Good 131
Perseverance Pays. 132
Humility Helps 134
Common Ground 136
Attitude, Attitude! 137
Determined Devin. 139
Is there a Song in Your Heart? 141
Believe in the Darkness 143
Coincidence or Christ? 145
Praying in the Shower. 148
It Worked Out Just Fine 150
Keep Praying! God uses Unlikely People. 151
Mercy 152
Running on Empty? 154
Be Encouraged! God is Faithful! 156
Noble Goals 157
Temper! Temper! Temper! 158
Seed Planter 160
Keep Moving Forward 162

More than One Way to Receive an Answer to Prayer........164
Confess the Ugly...................................166
Your Gift 168
Eyes on the Only Perfect Man to Ever Live.............. 170
Slow but Worth the Wait............................ 172
God Uses Imperfect People 173
Faith with Works is Active Faith......................175
Evidence 177
The Summary 179

Acknowledgements

No book is written and published without the help of others. I want to acknowledge the following people who helped make this dream a reality: my dad Thurman and mother Shirley for their love; my sisters Sue and Loretta (and her husband Eddie) and my brother Jeff (and his girlfriend Kim); my in-laws Harold and Virginia Markcum for their Christian commitment and kindness; actor Richard Thomas for his kindness and inspiration; my college instructor Gloria Baker for her inspiration, which sparked the idea behind this book; my sister-in-law Doreen, who has been a wonderful wife to my brother Bill; Debi and Glen; Angel and Fred; and to the memory of my brother-in-law Chuck.

I would be remiss if I did not remember my pastors from long ago, J.H. Ervin and Charles McEwen, who helped me in so many ways. Finally, I acknowledge Michael Caryl at Xulon Press Publishing for his dedication to this project, and Brandye Brixius for the same reason.

The Treasures of Darkness by Edwin L. Carpenter

Isaiah 45:2-3 says, "I will go before thee, and make the crooked places straight: I will break in pieces the gates of brass, and cut in sunder the bars of iron: And I will give thee the treasures of darkness, and hidden riches of secret places, that thou mayest know that I, the Lord, which call thee by thy name, am the God of Israel" (KJV).

Job 12:22 says, "He (God) discovereth deep things out of darkness, and bringeth out to light the shadow of death" (KJV).

Psalms 18:11 says, "He (God) made darkness his secret place; his pavilion round about him were dark waters and thick clouds of the skies" (KJV).

Dictionary.com gives a definition of darkness as "concealment"; the idea is secrecy. And another definition of treasure is "wealth of different forms" (Merriam Webster).

Think of this—God can bring treasures out of our dark places, out of our secret places of hurt and pain and disappointment. I picture it as finding treasure in a deep, dark cave after a long and tiring search.

In 1 Kings chapter 8, the Bible says that the priests could not stand as they ministered and dedicated Solomon's temple to the Lord. They were overwhelmed because His glory came down in a cloud, and it was dark all around them. They actually lay prostrate before the Lord. They could not see God, and yet God was all around them. It was dark, yet He was there with them—surrounding them with the glory cloud.

There are times when we cannot see God in our situations. We have been hurt by someone, or we are disappointed with our job or a relationship that has gone sour; we find ourselves dealing with more bills than money, or someone we loved has died. Yet God promises He will bring treasures to us out of our darkness.

In February 1986, I was the full-time associate minister of a church in Flint, Michigan. The funds of the church began to dry up, and it was a small church, under 100 members. With no warning or notice at all, I was told I would not be receiving a check anymore. My wife Jackie had just landed a job at a Ponderosa restaurant as a waitress, but we were still in a bind—with hardly any income during a freezing-cold February and with no prospects on the horizon. It was a dark place for us.

We prayed to God, and He began to bring treasures out of the darkness. My dear saintly grandmother, Emma, who is with the

Lord now, was blessed with some savings in the bank, and she insisted on paying our rent that February. After praying, I felt led to resign my position from the church. I knew I had completed my mission at this church. I was directed to another fellowship in the area, but before this, I began to receive speaking opportunities at various churches. I landed a part-time job at Sears, and between my wife's job, my part-time job, and the honorariums I received from speaking engagements, we survived and paid our bills. Later, I joined another fellowship, and a year later, I was a full-time senior pastor at a church in Greenville, Michigan, where we stayed for over six years. God truly brought treasures out of a dark time and place in our lives. 1 Corinthians 10:13 says that God is faithful, and He truly is.

> 2 Samuel 22:29 tells us, "For thou art my lamp, O Lord; and the Lord will lighten my darkness." The Lord lightened our darkness after the valley of losing my salary in Flint. Have you been recently walking in a dark place? God can lighten your darkness too.

Perhaps the greatest darkness we face is when we lose a loved one to the grave. I have lost a few very close people in my life—both of my grandparents who raised me, my father-in-law, and my dear father. The word "grief" does not do justice to the pain and sense of loss we feel during this breaking of a chain of a close relationship. A wise man once said that the strength of these ties to our loved ones is not truly felt until the bond is broken by death, and then we keenly feel the deepness of the relationship we shared with the departed loved one.

My wife's brother died unexpectedly several years ago, and it is even more heart-wrenching when the death is totally unexpected. He left a mother, three sisters, and two children behind. Anyone reading this knows how grief washes over you when you least expect it. You might hear a song on the radio that reminds you of your loved one. It might hit you like a hammer when you come across an old letter he/she sent you. It could simply be the mention of the person's name, and suddenly, grief floods your feelings like a rolling Niagara Falls. Yet God gives us treasures even in these moments. You feel the difference the person made in your life.

On December 26, 2006 President Gerald R. Ford, the 38th president of the United States, passed away. His body was flown to Grand Rapids, Michigan, for burial at the Gerald R. Ford Museum, following a funeral service in Washington, D.C. He was returned to the place he had grown up. Literally thousands of people flooded the museum to pay their last respects. Then, on Wednesday, January 3, 2006, a motorcade led the deceased president and his family to the Episcopal Church he had been married in to Betty so many years before for a private funeral. I was lined up on Fulton Street along with hundreds of others as we watched the motorcade pass us, nearing the church. People held signs saying such things as, "He was a great President," and almost everyone held or waved a flag. People waited as the hearse and the family in the motorcade returned some time later, turned off Fulton Street onto Monroe Avenue, and eventually found their way back a short distance away to the museum. The salutes continued at the burial service, and people continued to line the streets and pay honor to this man they revered as a hero.

A few days later, the family placed an ad in the *Grand Rapids Press*, thanking the thousands of people who had made their burden more bearable by the great display of love and honor they had displayed to the family, the former First Family of the United States. The Ford family had found some treasure in the dark places.

The last part of Psalms 30:5 says "weeping my endure for a night, but joy cometh in the morning" (KJV). This promise encourages us, telling us that there may be a time of grief and tears, but joy will return to our lives if we hang in there. Whatever you are facing in your life right now, remember this—God will bring treasures out of your darkness. I couldn't say it at the time, but I am glad now that I left that little church in Flint, Michigan. It is still struggling to this day, but we pastored a church in Greenville that grew from 25 people to 150! God had better things in store for me, but the treasures came from the darkness. He will lighten your journey too. Speaking of journeys, I hope you will join me for this one. Read on...

Treasures

Minister David B. Crabtree is a minister, and he once wrote, "A one-shot world is completely out of step with the God of the second chance. God's word paints graphic portraits of new beginnings. It is the story of grace." He also went on to write, rather humorously,

> My first toddling step was a stumble, my first swing at a ball was a strike, my first pour was a spill, my first kiss caused my first girlfriend to laugh out loud, my first bowling ball ended up in the gutter, my first drive on the golf course was a shank, my first fight was a loss, my first fish was not a keeper, my first job ended in termination, (and) my first article was kindly rejected (so was *mine*). (*Lead Pastor, Calvary Church,*N.D.)

Don't you shudder to think what life would be like without second chances? You could probably finish the following sentence: "If at first you don't succeed…" (try, try again)! Thank God Peter found out after he denied Christ that the Lord gives second chances (John 18:13-27 and John 21:17). Samson learned after his failure of revealing the secret of his strength to Delilah and sticking his toe into the lake of sin that God gives second chances (Judg. 16:28-30). And Job learned after his season of tears and loss that God gives second chances (Job 42:10). And Lazarus is the ultimate example that it isn't over until the Lord says it's over! (John 11: 43-44). He had been dead four days but was raised back to life. Talk about a second chance!

As mentioned elsewhere, but I will mention it here, because it speaks of a second chance for the famous evangelist, Billy Graham shared that he had a break-up with a girl that nearly broke his heart, but then he met Ruth, whose parents were missionaries to China, and they fell in love and were married; and together, they found happiness. They were married nearly sixty-four years. The prodigal son learned after wasting his inheritance with carnal living, drinking, and spending time with prostitutes that God gives second chances. He nearly starved, and the husks with which he fed the pigs began to look good to him. But he wizened up and decided to return home and to his father. Luke 15:11-32 tells of his story and how he returned to his father to find him waiting with open arms. His father greeted him with a kiss and called for a robe to be put on him, a ring on his finger (signifying he was still part of the family), and shoes on his feet. Then the father declared they would kill the fatted calf and celebrate. He was happy that his son, one who was dead spiritually, was alive again and that this precious lost son was now found. No one masters anything, including Christianity, the first time. But thank God He's the God of second chances.

Holmes and Watson and a Funny Moment

Sherlock Holmes and Dr. Watson went on a camping trip. After a good meal, they lay down for the night and went to sleep.

Some hours later, Holmes woke up, nudged his faithful friend, and said, "Watson, I want you to look up at the sky and tell me what you see."

Watson said, "I see millions and millions of stars."

Sherlock said, "And what does that tell you?"

After a minute or so of pondering, Watson said, "Astronomically, it tells me that there are millions of galaxies and potentially billions of planets. Horologically, I deduce that the time is approximately a quarter past three in the morning. Theologically, I can see that God is all-powerful and that we are small and insignificant. Meteorologically, I suspect that we will have a beautiful day today. What does it tell you?"

Holmes was silent for about thirty seconds and said, "Watson, you idiot! Someone has stolen our tent!" (Unknown author).

I love this joke because it reminds us that we need to stop and laugh sometimes. Laughter is a gift of God. Proverbs 17:22 says, "A merry heart doeth good like a medicine: but a broken spirit drieth the bones." Obviously, remembering to laugh or see the humorous side of life can help us combat the dark times we sometimes face. Have you laughed today?

A Smile Can Make a Big Difference

I once read about a young man who had committed suicide. In a note he had written, "If one person smiles at me today, I will not commit suicide." Apparently, no one did. I told this at our home church recently, and a lady named Joanna told me that she now makes an extra effort to smile at people when she is out and about. The story affected her. Sometimes, just a little thing as seemingly inconsequential as a smile can make someone's day. You can bring a treasure out of their darkness. You can make their day.

Love is All-Powerful

In May 2011, a young woman named Bethany Lansaw took cover in her bathtub during a tornado that devastated her home city of Joplin, Missouri. Her husband, Don, covered her body with his and took the blows from flying debris. He died, and she survived because of his love, courage, and heroism. She naturally wrestled with the question "Why?" But a year after the tornado, she said that she finds comfort because, "Even on the worst day of my life, I was loved." She said, "He sacrificed himself for me. If you talk to anybody who knows me, you know he wouldn't have wanted it any other way. As many times as people say that, it doesn't make it easier to comprehend. But I'm always going to remember him as my hero."(Kansas City Star, Kent Babb, 5-27-2011).

John 15:13 says, "Greater love hath no man than this, that a man lay down his life for his friends." Don Lansaw had that kind of love.

God will bring forth treasures from your darkness. Drive forward.

God Does Not Hold Back Good Things

I remember very vividly Easter of 1987. My wife really wanted a new Easter dress. She hadn't had one for a while, and during this particular time, I didn't think we could afford it. People who have never pastored small churches need to realize that sometimes you work a full or part-time job to supplement your income, and if you lose that extra job or if you feel led it is time to move on to another church, then it is easy to experience some financial difficulty. I was not one to waste money, and I wouldn't change my years of pastoring at various churches for anything. But the truth is, it can be a real challenge for a minister financially at times. Unless you pastor a very large church or are on TV, you don't get rich being a minister. We pastored in Greenville, Michigan, at the time my wife desired a new dress, and although I was full-time, the salary only met our basic needs.

My wife is not materialistic. She has worn used clothes and worn out some of the new ones she was able to purchase. But this particular year, it was just her heart's desire to buy a new Easter dress for Resurrection Day. And even though we couldn't afford it, God brought a treasure out of the darkness. Her mother, Virginia, decided that year that she was going to buy her three daughters—Angel, Debi, and Jackie—each a new Easter dress! My wife was so thrilled that she received her very heart's desire. And my in-laws, Harold and Virginia, attended Easter service with us that year. God revealed to Jackie that even in the dark place of financial struggle, He is able to bring treasures out of the dark places.

New York City, Wow!

I had a goal from the time I was about seventeen to travel to New York City. I would see the Statue of Liberty on TV, the Empire State Building, the World Trade Center, and the hustle and bustle of the busy city streets, and I longed to see it in person. I was raised in the country with a garden and even with chickens, a goat, a cow, and a pig. So, New York City looked like an amazing place to visit, a totally different world from my own.

It looked as if it would happen in the fall of 1987. A couple from our church in Greenville, Carl and Norma, knew the area well and planned to drive us there on vacation so Jackie and I could see it and so I could realize my dream. One problem—Carl had a history of heart problems and had a light heart attack and wound up recuperating that fall. I was twenty-seven at this time and had already waited for ten years for my ambition to be realized. I would have to wait a bit longer.

Jump ahead to the following spring, April 1988. I was twenty-eight years old. Carl was doing much better, and this time we were able to go. I could not believe my eyes as we neared the Statue of Liberty in a ferry, the beautiful green lady which was a gift to America from France. She loomed larger and larger as we drew closer and closer. I got a lump in my throat. I gazed up at her holding up her torch. I remember Jackie and I inspecting the pedestal and then climbing up to the crown, and I marveled at the spiraling staircase inside the statue as we walked the 354 steps (equivalent to 20 stories) to get to the top. Our legs grew rubbery as we neared the top, but we finally made it. It was a grand view looking out from the crown over New York Harbor. It was worth the climb to see it.

I also remember walking back down, and my wife was nervous because you could look over the side of the staircase and literally see all the way down to the bottom. "Please don't touch me!" she said nervously when I touched her back at one point. But we made it to safety. I have other wonderful memories too.

I remember eating at a three-story Burger King for lunch. We have just one-story Burger Kings in Michigan! I also remember spending over $8 for a hot dog and drink, and this was over thirty years ago! I recall hearing different foreign languages on the streets, such as Yiddish and Spanish. We also went up to the top floor, the summit, of the World Trade Center and looked out on an observation deck at the busy city below. It was breathtaking. I remember calling my dear grandmother from the World Trade Center so I could share my realized dream with her. "I'm in New York City!" I proclaimed over the phone. She was glad for me. We were typical tourists and took A LOT of photos. We also visited the legendary Empire State Building, but I never did spot King Kong.

Disappointments often lead to triumphs if we simply hang in there and wait. I had a wait of five months from the fall of '87 to the spring of '88 and a total eleven-year-wait after I first decided

I wanted to go in 1977. But someone once said if we change the first letter of the word "disappointment" to the letter "H" and make it "His appointment," everything will be okay. I like that. Waiting on the Lord in the darkness can lead to light and a realized dream.

The Empty Nest

"Lo, children are an heritage of the LORD: and the fruit of the womb is his reward" (Psalm 127:3).

This scripture is absolutely true. My wife Jackie and I have one child, Daniel, and raising him was like receiving a reward from both the Lord and my wife. I enjoyed being a dad. I still do. However, from the day the child is born, you know the day will come when he will move on.

The empty nest—that's what my wife Jackie and I experienced beginning on Friday, June 16, 2017. Our son, our only son Daniel, moved to Kalamazoo, almost an hour south from Grand Rapids. He had rented an apartment and was scheduled to be married on Saturday, July 15, 2017. I had heard the term "empty nest" before, but it became a painful reality to me.

Having been a full-time minister for much of Daniel's upbringing, I was—at times—Mr. Mom. He would frequently accompany me to church where he would claim a spot in the children's area to play while I took care of church business. Many times after my church hours, I would take him to lunch at Burger King or McDonald's. Frequently, we would stop at Schuler Books and enjoy an hour or so there. Quite often, I was the one who would pick him up from school, sometimes having driven him there that morning. So, a few days after his move to Kalamazoo or "Kazoo" (that's what the people who live there call it), I was noticing his lack of presence at home and in my life—very much so—to the point it hurt. I knew he wasn't going to pop in from a date with Kristen and head to his bedroom to play video games before going to sleep. He was gone.

Oh sure, I would see him every so often when he and Kristen would come to visit, but it would never be the same again. And I knew it. I often found myself stopping at his bedroom door, longing to see him in there. I made few changes to his room.

But God brought forth a treasure out of the darkness of my pain from the separation from my son. My wife Jackie and I, already close, grew even closer. We went out on more date nights and clung to one another when we experienced the mutual sadness of missing our son. It was almost as if we were starting over in our lives together.

Don't get me wrong. I still miss my son sometimes. I still occasionally stop at the door frame of his old bedroom and ask myself, "Where did the time go?" But the pain is a bit less now. Recently for Easter, his wife traveled out of state, and he spent the night with us and attended church with us Easter morning. It was a great experience to see him early Easter morning, asleep in his old room. I got to go back in time, albeit for a moment. Our God can bring treasures out of our pain—even the pain of an empty nest.

It's New!

When I pastored in Reed City from 2009 to 2012, the church wasn't new. The church had been established for many years, and the building was built in 1959, the same year that I was born. I wasn't sure if the building was in better shape or if I was. The building was actually in good shape, but despite the fact it was an older church, it was new to me. I remember going through old records and names and determining where the church was in terms of membership and current ministries. I knew the congregation was looking to me to bring something new to the church—a fresh vitality and a new direction.

I like the word *new*. Revelation 21:5 mentions Christ seated on the throne, and He says, "I am making everything new." What a great image that conjures up—when Christ returns one day, everything will be new, and everyone who is part of His kingdom will have a fresh start and a new home. I am reminded of an old song, "Wait'll You See My Brand New Home"(Joe E. Parks, Songs of Inspiration No.2).Of course, it refers to our future heavenly home. It is always nice to purchase something new—a new coat or some new clothes, a new TV, a new home, and so on. Many times, we have had to put up with the old more than we care to, but when we finally get the *new*, it is a thrilling experience. I recall reading about a pastor who was going to move from the home he had lived in for many years. He was now elderly. As he stopped to reflect before exiting the old house, a young man sensed the pastor's hesitancy and said, "Don't worry, Pastor, your new home is better than your old one." One day our new home will be much better than anything we have here. While we are here, God often opens up a new experience or a new blessing to us just because He wants to bring light into our lives so that it will overtake the darkness.

A Spunky Daughter-in-Law

I used to pray over my son Daniel when he was young, still at home, and asleep at night. I would wander into his bedroom, stand next to his bed, and pray for his future wife—that she would be devoted and committed to him and love him for who he is. God answered that prayer by sending our daughter-in-law, Kristen, into his life. They were married on July 15, 2017, and she has stood with him during the good and the bad. They have already experienced prosperous times and lean times as well.

I love my son with all my heart, but even he would agree that he occasionally needs a kick between his back pockets! Recently, he and Kristen spent a Saturday night in order to attend Easter service with us Sunday morning, and my wife Jackie and I could not get him out of the bed Easter morning no matter how many times we called his name. He is a night owl and loves to sleep in when the rest of us are up and about. Kristen finally marched upstairs, and within minutes, he came down. She knew how to get him moving!

It was difficult for us when Daniel moved away from home in June 2017. He is our only child. But we delight in seeing that he has a loving and caring wife (and spunky!) to stand with him, and she truly does. God filled our loneliness from missing our son to our fulfillment in now having a daughter. God brings light out of the dark places of our loneliness.

Climbing out of Holes

Have you ever felt as if you are attempting to climb out of a hole? Joseph was placed in one, but God brought him out. Some years ago, not long before I ministered to a congregation at Reed City, I had been laid off from my job (this has happened to me more than once), and I was working a part-time job while my wife was full-time as a receptionist at ITT Technical Institute. We needed our garage roof repaired, and we were in a bit of a financial hole. Yet a fellow Christian offered to fix it and have us give him a down payment and pay it off as we could. The total bill was $1,175, and I was pleased that we pretty quickly got it down to $275, and then shortly after that, we paid it off.

How do you deal with "being in a hole"? Do you complain? Do you remain positive? Do you tackle it with a "can-do" attitude? Jackie and I have learned to trust the Lord and to rejoice even in small victories. We began to climb out of the hole, and God helped. Soon, I landed the full-time pastorate position at the church in Reed City, and we ministered there for a few years. People like Dan and Dawne Dack and their kids encouraged us. God ALWAYS will send someone along to encourage you. They had a son named

Caleb that really took a liking to me and I did to him as well. Who are you grateful for in your life today?

You may occasionally face the darkness of a hole, but there is light at the end of that tunnel or, in this case, the hole. The same God who brought Joseph out of the pit will do the same for you. Hebrews 13:8 says that Jesus Christ is the "same yesterday, and today, and forever."

Jingle Bells at a Funeral?!

Matthew 5:41 in the King James Bible says, "And whosoever shall compel thee to go a mile, go with him twain (two)." In other words, go the extra mile.

That reminds me of the story of a minister and his wife that had known a couple for many years. They were now getting up in years, and the minister's friend died, leaving behind his wife. The wife asked the minister if he would not only conduct the funeral service for her husband but if he would sing the man's favorite song, "Jingle Bells." The minister wasn't sure if he misunderstood. So, he repeated the song to the woman, "You want me to sing 'Jingle Bells'?"

"That's right," the lady replied.

The minister thought it was very unusual, especially considering that it wasn't even Christmastime. But he cared for the dear woman so he replied that yes, he would sing the song at his friend's funeral.

He admitted he felt a bit foolish as he started off, "Dashing through the snow, in a one-horse open sleigh…" But he sang the song, "Jingle bells, jingle bells, jingle all the way…oh what fun it is to ride in a one-horse open sleigh." (James Lord Pierpont, 1857)

After the funeral, the deceased man's wife came up to the minister and asked, "Did I ask you to sing 'Jingle Bells'?"

"Why yes, you did," replied the minister.

"Oh, I'm so sorry," replied the woman. "I meant 'When They Ring Those Golden Bells'!"

Sometimes, we are asked to go the extra mile in helping someone. It may not be easy. It might even be a bit awkward, but this minister now owns a memory which can bring a smile to his face. He did his best to go the extra mile. Do you?

Laughter Helps

When we are honest, people will remember us during the difficult times of our lives. When we sow honesty, we reap respect and trustworthiness.

During the Civil War, we were fortunate to have Abraham Lincoln as our sixteenth president. I have looked at photos of President Lincoln from the beginning of his presidency to the final known photograph taken of him just before he was assassinated by John Wilkes Booth. The lines and wrinkles speak of the stressful years and the toll that the war took on him. He looked like two separate men just years apart, one younger and one much older. He aged considerably during the intervening years of his presidency. Yet he is not only remembered today for the hardships he endured during the Civil War, which nearly split our nation apart, but he also is remembered as "Honest Abe."

It has been said he once walked several miles during a cold winter month to return a book he had borrowed from a friend.

I love the story I read about a phone call that a minister received. The phone rang, and Rev. O'Malley picked up the receiver. "Hello," said a voice on the other end of the line, "is this Rev. O'Malley?"

"It is," he replied.

"This is the IRS. Can you help us?"

"I can," replied the good reverend.

"Do you know a Ted Houlihan?" asked the agent.

"I do," he replied.

"Is he a member of your congregation?"

"He is," replied the minister.

"Did he donate $10,000 to your church?" There was a long pause.

"He will," replied the minister. (Anonymous).

God brings good things out of the dark places when we are people of integrity and character. We will be remembered that way, just as Honest Abe is. Proverbs 22:1 says "A good name is rather to be chosen than great riches, and loving favour rather than silver and gold."

Call 9-1-1

"He that dwelleth in the secret place of the most High shall abide under the shadow of the Almighty" (Psalm 91:1).

Most people know that dialing 9-1-1 in America will connect you with emergency help. I have read about children saving family members by using this quite familiar phone number. The three numbers are easy to remember. At least, they usually are. I remember my dear grandmother, Emma, once repeating to my wife and I her attempt at it, and she kept wanting to say, "9-1-9," but she eventually got it right, "9-1-1."

This Psalm 91:1 is our biblical 9-1-1. It speaks of our Most High God and that He is the Almighty. And we can abide in His shadow. He casts a long and a welcome shadow. As a shadow or shade protects one from the sun, our God is our protector in the time of trouble.

I read about a mother who had her infant son in her car, strapped into the back seat. A man hijacked her car, and she was forced to stay in the car along with her son. The hijacker didn't know it, but she quietly dialed 9-1-1 on her cell phone, and the police dispatcher was able to overhear the conversation. The woman spoke with the thief and purposely made mention of their location so as to alert the police. Sure enough, in a short amount of time, she was rescued, and she and her son were safe. To give another analogy, trail walkers in Colorado often get lost, and many times, they only have one bottle of water and are wearing shorts and a T-shirt. Thankfully, the Alpine Rescue team has rescued many of them, some as they have attempted to climb a mountain. When we look to the God of Psalm 91:1, He will rescue us and answer our prayers.

Psalms 46:1 says, "God is our refuge and our strength, a very present help in trouble." I remember being in surgery on August 17, 2010. I had suffered a heart attack, as mentioned elsewhere in this book, and my surgeon, Dr. Foster, was attempting to put one to two stents in my heart. He was trying to go through my groin to get to my heart, but someone pulled out the sheath in my groin too quickly, and I began to hemorrhage. I became sick to my stomach as I looked at the heart monitor and saw my heart rate drop to thirty-two beats per minute. I remember praying in my heart and mind, "Please God, don't let me die." Dr. Foster yelled at a few helpers to get on top of my groin and to get the bleeding to stop. I thought of my wife and seventeen-year-old son. Thankfully, they were able to get the bleeding stopped, and my heart rate began to climb again.

The next day, the doctor successfully put two stents in, and some days later when he attempted a third, he was amazed because my other blockage had opened up and wasn't bad enough to warrant a third stent. I wanted to add to my previous story about my heart attack because some blessings did come out of that difficult period I went through. So, I got out of surgery early. Now, every year on August 17, my wife and I celebrate "Celebration of Life Day" because I am still here, and believe me, I am thankful to be.

I still remember my sister-in-law Debbie telling Dr. Foster when she learned I didn't need the third stent, "He's a minister you know. That's a miracle of God!" And it was.

When you need to call on God for emergency help, remember 9-1-1, Psalms 91:1, which states He is the Most High and the Almighty. God will bring a treasure out of your dark place.

Placed Here for a Reason

God truly works all things together for good. His Word says in Romans 8:28, "And we know that in all things God works for the good of those who love him, who have been called according to his purpose" (NIV).

After I moved on from pastoring a church in Reed City in 2012, I had to take two difficult jobs in order to simply survive and pay the bills. A pastor's life is seldom trouble-free. I worked for a while at a bank in customer service, taking calls and helping customers with their banking needs and with issues such as late fees. Anyone that has ever worked in customer service knows it is not an easy job. I had to deal with angry and, at times, hostile customers who were upset with the bank for one reason or another. I had people hang up on me. I had people use strong language while speaking to me. I had to remember they were thinking of me as the bank, not as Edwin Carpenter.

Yet on two occasions, I had customers call that had late fees, and both of the ladies were so distraught over their financial situations that they mentioned suicide. I encouraged both of them to talk to someone, perhaps a pastor, and to get to a church, and I truly believe I helped both of them. No one else I spoke with at the bank received a call like that. I took comfort in knowing that I was God's messenger of comfort to those two ladies at that time.

The other job I moved onto when the door closed at the bank was working at Amway in Ada, Michigan. I worked on a product line in addition to skid loading. I had very little factory experience and no skid loading experience to speak of. There were days when I lifted 400 boxes or more. Some of the product lines moved with great speed, and when I first started the job, I would become frustrated trying to keep up with those speedy lines.

In addition, I had too many would-be bosses. One person would tell me how he or she thought I should do the job, and then someone else would come along and tell me a totally different way to do it! On one product line, I was required to walk fast to keep up, going back and forth between one end of the line and the other in order to take care of two different jobs. One of the jobs was to provide boxes of tubes to a person to place on the product line. I literally had over ten people tell me in a short amount of time as they walked by not to forget to move fast and to remember the tubes at the other end of the line. After hearing it over and over, I admit it got to me. I remember grabbing a box that needed to be torn up, ripping it with all my might, and thrusting it into a bin in anger and frustration. A fellow worker walked up to me and asked, "Is everything all right?" Yet something good came out of my work experience while at Amway. I met two fellow Christians, John and Amy, and we became good friends during this difficult season in our lives. My wife Jackie and I would have them over, go to their home, and out to dinner. We even spent a few New Years' Eves together. We encouraged and supported one another.

As with some friendships, they are no longer in our lives, but it was for a specific season, and it was something good that came out of working at a place that sometimes frustrated me. And I met some other terrific people there that I am still Facebook friends with to this day. Once again, God brought treasures out of my dark places.

Changing Seasons

Ecclesiastes 3:1-8 says:

¹ To every thing there is a season, and a time to every purpose under the heaven:

² A time to be born, and a time to die; a time to plant, and a time to pluck up that which is planted;

³ A time to kill, and a time to heal; a time to break down, and a time to build up;

⁴ A time to weep, and a time to laugh; a time to mourn, and a time to dance;

⁵ A time to cast away stones, and a time to gather stones together; a time to embrace, and a time to refrain from embracing;

⁶ A time to get, and a time to lose; a time to keep, and a time to cast away;

⁷A time to rend, and a time to sew; a time to keep silence, and a time to speak;

⁸A time to love, and a time to hate; a time of war, and a time of peace.

The above passage of Scripture guarantees us that if we have gone through a time of adversity, it will eventually change. Like the changing seasons, winter will give way to spring and then summer. If we have wept for a season, a time of laughter will soon be ours. If we have mourned, our time to dance is coming!

In Psalms 30:11, the psalmist writes, "Thou has turned for me my mourning into dancing..."

On February 10, 1999, my grandmother who had raised me, Emma Fornash, passed away. I navigated my way through a time of grief and mourning. At times, I would cry in my car while driving because I missed her so much. It wasn't until six months later, in August, that I truly began to heal. People who have lost a loved one via death will tell you that you never completely get over it, and that's true. I still get teary-eyed to this day at times when I mention her or think of her. But I began to finally heal from the deep grieving after six months. I felt like I could truly live again. My wife Jackie and our six-year-old son Daniel and I took a vacation to New York City. We stayed in the now (sadly) gone World Trade Center. We visited the city and had a blast. We laughed—I laughed—again. It felt good. God had turned my mourning into dancing. The man who puts our bulletin out at church every week, Jim Groendyke, once put this in the bulletin: "Life isn't about waiting for the storm to pass. It's about learning to dance in the rain." How difficult that can be, but what a statement of faith! When we dance during the storm, we are stating that we know all is well because God is in charge. But if we can't find it in ourselves to dance during certain storms, like when we're grieving, we can take courage in the fact that God will heal our hurts and that we will dance to a joyous tune again. God can turn our despair into dancing.

Psalms 30:5 tells us that "weeping may endure for a night, but joy cometh in the morning."

Mentors

P aul was a mentor and a role model to young minister Timothy, whom he called his son in the faith (1 Tim. 1:2).

We all need mentors that can help us grow, especially when we hit rough patches and go through difficult times. My first pastor was J.H. Ervin, who pastored Faith Temple Church in Brighton, where I grew up. It is the same church in which I found the Lord, met my wife Jackie, and married her, and I was called to preach there. Rev. Ervin left a big first impression on me—he preached the Bible with passion and fire. By the time I was called to be a minister, Charles McEwen was the pastor, a happy and loud man who wasn't ashamed to serve the Lord with praise. He gave me my first opportunities to speak, and I will forever be grateful to him. I have also followed a few TV ministers and read some good books written by them. I particularly remember listening to a minister that encouraged people a lot. It seemed to be his gift.

I recall a time when I needed some encouragement. I had been full-time at the church I pastored in Wayland for many years, and I loved it. I loved having plenty of time to read and put sermons together, pray, and visit the sick. But some of our people retired, some moved, and some simply moved on, and suddenly, I had to take a salary cut. I needed to find work to supplement my income and provide for my family. Sometimes, we need to be challenged to do better in our spiritual walk by the preaching of God's Word, but, friend, there are times we need to be encouraged too. There is a place for both, and I believe we need to keep that balance.

During the summer of 2004, I landed a job as an enrollment counselor at a local college. I began first contacting prospective students. I had to be on the phone a lot and do a bit of a sales pitch, and it wasn't a job I enjoyed very much. Not long into my job, there was a change of supervisors, and I wound up with a man with a military background named Len, and he didn't seem to have much of a sense of humor. I am not speaking unkindly of our military. I appreciate them very much. But this individual ran the office like a drill sergeant and not a very nice one. As I learned more on the job and began to actually meet with students, he didn't help me much. He seemed to dislike me. He would take good leads and give them to others. He put pressure on me to enroll more students. One morning after one of my newly enrolled students didn't show up for his first class the night before, he totally placed the blame on me. I was miserable.

I continued to pray, to watch the minister who encouraged me (and I needed it at the time), and to trust God. Eventually, I landed a job with The Dove Foundation (now Dove.org), and it wound up being one of my favorite jobs. I got to review DVDs and movies, promoting wholesome, family films as well as faith-based films. I started out as an associate editor for the website and then was promoted to editor. I was able to see fantastic films like *Facing the Giants* weeks before the premiere. I interviewed some wonderful people, such as Alex Kendrick, a writer and star of *Facing the Giants*. I interviewed Ken Wales, a producer of the remarkable film *Amazing Grace: The Story of William Wilberforce*. He was a delight to speak with, and his terrific film about a man who stood against slavery long before Lincoln did during the Civil War was a true inspiration.

But the encouragement I received from this TV minister/author was so appreciated. Sometimes, TV preachers get a bum rap, and I am the first to admit that some put too much emphasis on asking for money for the ministry. But it is so important to look to good, solid Bible teachers and preachers and to read books which will encourage you. We all need mentors. I eventually met this particular preacher in person, and he signed his book for me, and I was able to tell him he had helped me. If I mentioned his name, you would probably know him, but I want God to receive the glory; so I will just say his encouragement was greatly appreciated. Look what happened as Timothy followed Paul's amazing teaching. There are two books in the Bible named 1 Timothy and 2 Timothy! He grew and became a spiritual rock himself, much like his mentor Paul. When we study, we grow, and when we grow, we are used of God, and when we are used of God, we can mentor others.

Journey's End

Journey's end—doesn't that sound great? Various images come to my mind, including a high school or college graduate at the graduation ceremony, a young man or woman leaving home for the first time, the end of the work life and a welcome retirement, and, well, you get the idea. We have certain travels or journeys in this life which also come to an end. The ultimate end is when we die, and as actor Richard Thomas once said to me, that might be the biggest surprise of all! But for those who trust in the Lord, it will all be good.

I have been a Superman fan for many years. There are a lot of Christian types or symbols in his story. Think about it—a father that loves his son enough to send him to earth to help save people? There have been many manifestations of the story of Superman, such as comic books, movies, and TV shows. One that my wife Jackie, son Daniel, and I all enjoyed was the TV series *Smallville*.

The show finally ended after a ten-year run. The premise of the series was Clark Kent's journey as he moved toward becoming the Man of Steel. Over the years, young Clark attended high school, struggled with his developing powers and strength and speed, and fell for Lana Lang, a beautiful girl who attended Smallville High School. He eventually met Lois Lane and landed a job at the *Daily Planet*. In this version of the TV series, all of this happened *before* he became Superman. A lot of anticipation was built up by fans who had followed Clark Kent's journey from the beginning. They couldn't wait for the moment when he would don the suit with the big "S" emblazoned on his chest to finally become Superman. He would have reached the culmination of his journey—he would have become Superman. Yet if this had happened early in the series, say by the end of the first season, there would not have been any more stories to tell about his journey in becoming Superman. The series would have ended. It was not a series about Superman but about Clark Kent becoming Superman.

My family watched the finale with great anticipation. We wanted the pay-off, to see him become Superman and fly. But without those ten years of the journey, the destiny would never have been reached. So, it is with life. Life is really more about the journey than it is about the climax or "journey's end." In the final episode, Clark Kent (Tom Welling) did indeed become Superman. We saw him fly to rescue Lois who was trapped in a plane that was going down. We saw him do the "shirt pull" at the very conclusion, in which we saw the "S" on the chest. He was about to fly off to rescue people from a bomb in a building. We knew one journey had ended, and another had begun.

Ironically, I never dreamed that my wife Jackie and I would get to meet two of the stars of the show, Tom Welling who played Clark Kent and Michael Rosenbaum who played his nemesis, arch-villain Lex Luthor. But we did meet them both in 2018. Michael was a delight, coming off stage to put his arm around me and walk down the aisle as he personally answered a question about which guest stars he enjoyed working with. Then at the photo op we got with Tom, since we had seen him just a short while before and had spoken with him, I joked and said, "We're practically family now."

"What time is dinner?" he asked, and Jackie, Tom, and I all laughed at his joke.

The Bible says in Luke 19:13 that we should "occupy" till Christ returns, or in other words, continue on our journey, doing what we need to do, the necessary things. The climax will come. Christ will return. But we need to continue in our journey to get to that wonderful moment. The journey will end—but it is more about the journey than the journey's end. But when Christ returns, it will be the ultimate journey's end.

Here is an epitaph on a tombstone: A marker seen in Hatfield, Massachusetts:

Beneath this stone
>A lump of clay
>Lies Arabella Young
>Who on the 21st of May
>1771
>Began to hold her tongue.

Other Epitaphs: In a London, England cemetery:
>Ann Mann
>Here lies Ann Mann,
>Who lived an old maid
>But died an old Mann.
>Dec. 8, 1767

The Treasures of Darkness

On the grave of Ezekiel Aikle in East Dalhousie Cemetery, Nova Scotia:
>Here lies
>Ezekial Aikle
>Age 102
>The Good Die young.

Playing with names in a Ruidoso, New Mexico, cemetery:
>Here lies
>Johnny Yeast
>Pardon me
>For not rising.

Oops! Harry Edsel Smith of Albany, New York:
>Born 1903--Died 1942
>Looked up the elevator shaft to see if
>the car was on the way down. It was.

In a Thurmont, Maryland, cemetery:
>Here lies an Atheist
>All dressed up
>And no place to go (Funny Epitaphs Website).

Mmmm...Arabella Young, Ezekiel Aikle, and Johnny Yeast were not well thought of. What would be your epitaph if you were to die soon? On my grandmother's tomb the words, "Beloved Wife and Mother" are inscribed. These are lovely roles and thoughts to be sure. Can you think of a compliment you have received, such as that you are pretty or handsome or a talented singer, musician, hard worker, etc.? Someone once said that what we are is God's gift to us, and what we become is our gift to Him. You may go through difficult times, but if you have ever received a word of encouragement or appreciation or a compliment, that is indeed a treasure. On headstones, there is usually the date of a person's birth and death, and a dash in between those two is placed. The most important part is the dash, which signifies what we did with our life, our "journey," if you will. What will your dash stand for? What kind of life will you have lived? And will your stone possibly say, "Beloved Wife and Mother" or, "on the 21st of May, began to hold her tongue"?

A Nice Conclusion

---◆---

It has been stated by more than one person that life isn't so much about the destination but about the journey that we take to get to our destiny. There is definitely some truth in that thought, although I would hate to journey on for a long time and miss the destination! The destination is very important. But without the journey, we would never arrive at our destiny. I mentioned this regarding the Superman character in this book, and it is a universal story, true of other characters and heroes.

In an old TV series that I watched as a kid and loved, *The Guns of Will Sonnett*, a western, Walter Brennan, as Will Sonnett, had raised his grandson Jeff (Dack Rambo) from an infant. Will's son and Jeff's father, Jim (Jason Evers), had left home shortly after Jeff was born. Jim had gained the reputation (undeservedly) as a quick gun and a gun fighter after Jeff's mother had passed away. As the series opened, Jeff had grown up and told his grandfather, "I have to go find my father."

The series ran for two years, and it was about the journey that the grandfather, Will, and the grandson, Jeff, took to find Jeff's father, Jim. They had close calls where they just missed Jim. They

A Nice Conclusion

almost caught up with him on several occasions, only to just miss out. As a viewer, it kept me coming back week after week to see if they would ever find Jim Sonnett. Several stories focused on the bad guys trying to prove how fast they were by challenging Jim Sonnett. He hated to kill and hated to use his gun, but he had to defend himself several times.

Finally, as season two wound down, there was a show that aired, "Three Stand Together" that showed Will and Jeff finally catch up to Jim Sonnett. Jeff rode up on his horse to meet Jim, sitting on his horse with his rifle ready, waiting to see who this young man was. The show was well-directed, with Jeff riding up a slope with great anticipation to finally meet his father at the top of the hill. Jim had no idea who Jeff was. Then came the moment, the destiny moment, when Jeff looked at Jim's searching eyes, and said, "Hello, Pa." And it dawned on Jim that this was his son. They both got off their horses and embraced. The show's ending was fantastic, with Will, his son Jim, and grandson Jeff all becoming lawmen in a town called Samson. What a reunion! They were finally together, father Will and son Jim and father Jim and son Jeff.

I had not seen this show in many years, and a few years back, I finally got to see it again. At the climax when Jeff and Jim met, I had bittersweet feelings. On the one hand, Jeff had reached his goal. He had found his father! On the other hand, I knew the journey was over. There would be no more shows about the search for his father. Indeed, "Three Stand Together" was the last show. But it featured a joyful ending, a reward for the audience. Jesus tells us when he returns, in Revelation 22:12, that His reward will be with Him. He will reward us for following Him, for journeying with Him. And our destiny will be grand! Our journey in this life is sometimes peppered with troubles and hardships, but the destiny will make the journey seem trivial. Dare to reach your destiny! But do try to enjoy the journey along the way.

The Hardship of Ministry

2 Timothy 2:3 says:
> ³Thou therefore endure hardness, as a good soldier of Jesus Christ.

This verse makes it clear—ministry can be difficult, challenging, and hard. A pastor used to have a reply to people that commented about encountering a difficult moment while doing the Lord's work, "Welcome to ministry!" and he would smile.

I remember my old Sunday School teacher that I had as a boy. His name was Charles, but he was elderly and kind, and everyone referred to him as "Uncle Charlie." My brother and I enjoyed him as our teacher for a few years, and he used to refer to us as his best students because we took such an interest in his teaching of God's Word. He dealt with health issues but showed up week after week to teach the class. Today, both my brother and I are ordained ministers. "Uncle Charlie" endured difficult times, but due to his faithfulness, my brother and I are fruit of his ministry.

I read once about a man that wanted very much to be a missionary. He was turned down by the mission's board the first time he applied for they felt he wasn't ready as he was inexperienced.

He got offered a chance to be an assistant missionary. He was disappointed but accepted this offer. As time passed, his obvious calling became very evident, and he eventually went to the field as a full-fledged missionary. Enduring difficulty has its rewards with the passing of time. A person that never quits cannot fail.

There have been times that I have been checking out at a register at a grocery store and had my phone ring, a call from a church member that needed guidance or help. At times, I have had my dinner interrupted due to a need by someone in the church. I remember watching the Pistons about to win the NBA Championship in 1990, and I had to leave to visit a member that had just been admitted into the hospital. Ministry is not always convenient, but it is worthwhile. For example, I have received phone calls from young women who were girls in churches that I pastored, and they were now grown and about to get married. They were calling me to perform their wedding ceremonies. That is rewarding beyond description.

Likewise, I have had former church members send me letters or post nice things on Facebook, saying I influenced them and helped them. Those kinds of letters and posts cannot be measured in respect to the satisfaction they have given me—in knowing I was an instrument of God to have touched their lives. Some people may believe that pastors have it easy, only preaching twice a week. But for those who really are in the know, they realize that pastors are on call, they study a lot, they go to hospitals and pray with hurting people, they comfort mourning people at funerals, and they do their best while at times putting up with criticism. Ministry isn't always easy, even if you are not a pastor but a Sunday School teacher, a musician, an administrator, board member, etc. But in the long run, we are called of God, and it is worth it.

Blood is Thicker than Water

If you ever experience a rough day and—let's face it—we all have, it often helps to remember the people God has placed in your life. In this case, I am speaking of family. Although I was raised alone by my grandparents, Henry and Emma Fornash, I still had a relationship with my twin brother Bill, my older sister Sue, and my younger sister Loretta. Then, on the 4th of July, 1969, my youngest brother Jeff was born. I am grateful for my four siblings.

My twin brother Bill is very much like me in many ways. He and I even start to say the same sentence at times. We both love the Detroit Tigers and many of the same TV shows. However, we differ in some respects. He likes baked beans, and I don't care for them much. I like green peppers on pizza, and he doesn't. Yet we are both ministers and both have pastored churches, and the small differences keep our relationship interesting.

My sister Sue is funny, outgoing, and kind. My sister Loretta is thoughtful, caring, and can really talk (but I love her)! My younger brother Jeff rides motorcycles and looks tough but has a heart of gold. What characteristics do your family members have that you love?

My daughter-in-law Kristen says her mother Robin is very kind but direct, and she's the one you want to go with you to return an item at the store! She takes no gruff. Her dad loves the outdoors and the water and is kind and a humble soul. No one person possesses all the same qualities, and that's good. Sometimes we need one thing and sometimes another quality to brighten our days. And so often, a loved one says something or does something that helps when we go through the dark places and the valleys.

My sister-in-law Angel is the kind that will knit a gift for someone over a period of months. My sister-in-law Debi is a person who sees what needs to be done, and she does it! She's a go-getter. My deceased brother-in-law Chuck was an intelligent "A" student, and my last memory of him is that he gave my wife and I some food from his pizza place to take with us after we visited him.

My brother-in-law Fred loves to travel, and he can talk about nature and beautiful places in this country all day long. Finally, my brother-in-law Glen is a hard worker and sometimes will see a side of a conversation that someone else wouldn't think of.

What quality do you need today? Turn to family for some light when you need it. They may make you laugh, tell you what you already know to be true, or just simply listen to you. But make no mistake about it, we need our family, and a brother (or sister) is born for the day of adversity (Prov. 17:17).

Meeting some Neat People

I have been fortunate to meet several actors that I grew up admiring on TV. Some of these opportunities presented themselves from my having worked as a writer at The Dove Foundation. God will give you the desires of your heart if you believe He can and if you do what you can about it. Psalms 84:11 says He will withhold no good thing from those that walk uprightly before Him. You may face a dark period when it is not happening—or a dream seems far away—but believe and keep trying!

I have often been inspired by actors who played "good guy" or hero roles, such as Richard Thomas when he played the aspiring writer John-Boy in *The Waltons*. Richard won an Emmy Award for his portrayal on this dramatic TV show about a struggling, close-knit family during the Depression years. I mentioned how I met him and interviewed him on the phone in another place in this book. I also met Alan Trammell, the World Series hero of the 1984 Detroit Tigers' World Championship team. He won gold gloves for his position at shortstop and was a very good hitter. He is my favorite Tiger from that '84 team, although all of them are terrific guys. He was as nice as could be, and it was a joy to meet him.

I met Adam West, who played the hero Batman on the classic *Batman* TV series from the sixties, on a few occasions. Adam always had a great voice as Batman and played it straight, although he had several instances where he got to let his humor shine through a bit. Watching Batman as a kid, with Batman climbing up the side of a building with the bat rope or punching the lights out of a snarling villain or blazing down the street in the utterly cool and sleek Batmobile, was a delight. The thing I noticed about Adam, who sadly just passed away on June 9, 2017, was that he loved to bring a smile to his fans and to the people he met. He was an easygoing man that was always upbeat when meeting people that loved him as Batman. He once saw my son Daniel, who was around seven at the time, with a bag of almonds and tried to sneak a few from Daniel, which made Daniel look up in surprise and made Adam laugh with delight. Adam once told my brother Bill and I to excuse him for a moment as he had to go to the "Bat room." Too funny.

The point is, what dream or goal or heart's desire have you been waiting on? Maybe it seems hopeless right now. But remember, the Lord holds back no good thing from those that please Him. It may seem dark at this moment, but believe and keep trying!

Burdens and Buried Treasure

Galatians 6:2:
> ² Bear ye one another's burdens, and so fulfil the law of Christ.

Sharing the hidden burdens we sometimes carry is important. It can help lighten our load. And sharing what God did to turn our hardships around is also important. I recently read that in March 1974, Chinese farmers made an amazing and surprising discovery. They found the Terracotta Army, life-size terracotta sculptures that actually date back to the third century BC. Discovered in this fantastic find were approximately 8,000 soldiers and 150 cavalry horses, in addition to 130 chariots which were drawn by 520 horses. It is now a very popular tourist site and is a kind of "buried treasure" that has been discovered.

The "buried treasure" we carry, our hidden burdens and dark places, can be brought to life and we can find relief—relief by a friend who lends an ear or a family member that encourages us. That is why it can be considered a buried "treasure" because it can connect us to others and we can later share how God unburdened us. God always has a light for us to encourage us in our dark places, and sometimes, He uses people to help be an instrument of that relief. If you are burdened today, can you think of someone to share the burden with?

Pray About Everything!

Philippians 4:6 says, "Be careful for nothing; but in every thing by prayer and supplication with thanksgiving let your requests be made known unto God."

When Paul wrote "in everything," he meant just that. We need to talk with God when things are going well and when they are not, when we have a need or we're disappointed in a situation or someone. Prayer really does change things. So often we hear that prayers will be answered in "God's time," and that is true. However, sometimes God's time is quick time!

For example, a couple I know named Kevin and Taylor who, along with their daughters Rylee and Jada, had bought a new home and moved into it, but their old home had not sold after a few months. They were making two house payments, and that was hard on their budget. Now, a couple of months may sound like a bit of time, but what is amazing is how quickly the tide turned and the situation was solved. One Sunday morning at church, I mentioned to our congregation that we needed to pray for their house to sell quickly. We prayed as a church, and that very week, they received an offer and their old house sold! Sometimes, corporate prayer or enlisting the prayers of others can help. But the point is—the situation changed quickly after prayer. C. H. Spurgeon once said, "Seasons of great need call for frequent seasons of prayer. Have a pleading heart and God will have a plenteous hand" (The Treasury of David, Kregel, 2004). In other words, God has plentiful answers to our plentiful prayers. He will be generous with His answers.

Waiting and walking by faith can be wearisome. But God can change the situation in the wink of an eye. He can bring treasures out of our darkness.

Temporary Obstacles

2 Corinthians 12:9 says, "⁹ And he said unto me, My grace is sufficient for thee: for my strength is made perfect in weakness. Most gladly therefore will I rather glory in my infirmities, that the power of Christ may rest upon me" (KJV).

"Temporary obstacles"—that's what obstacles are when you serve God. Think of Moses. He was slow of speech. He stammered when he spoke, and yet God told him to go to Pharaoh and demand that he set God's people free. Isn't it just like God to send someone with a speech impediment to speak on His behalf? That's because when we are weak, then we are strong because God's grace rests upon us. God became angry with Moses when Moses argued with God that he couldn't do it. God told him he would send Aaron with Moses to help be a mouthpiece. When God calls us to do something, He doesn't want excuses!

Yet we are human, and sometimes we feel inadequate when we go to do something for the Lord. I remember once when I was a young minister in training that our pastor asked my father-in-law to sing a song. My father-in-law hesitated, saying, "I can't remember all the words."

"I can do all things through Christ which strengthens me," quoted the pastor from Philippians 4:13.

"But I don't *remember the words*!" emphasized my father-in-law, Harold. But he went ahead, and do you know what happened? He got through the entire song and *did* remember all the words. Then he beamed at Pastor Chuck and said, "I *can* do all things through Christ which strengthens me!"

Moses and the Hebrews faced the Red Sea. Talk about an obstacle! Pharaoh pursued them and was not far behind them; the mountains were to the left and right of them, and the Red Sea loomed in front of them. But it was a temporary obstacle. For as Moses stretched forth his hand, God sent a mighty wind that parted the Red Sea, and the people crossed over on dry ground. For David, the giant Goliath was a temporary obstacle that was brought down by David's faith in God and his trusty slingshot. The Empire State Building fell, and little David stood tall. Don't be discouraged by an obstacle which lies in your path. God will get you past it somehow. He will give you another treasure out of the darkness.

The Fonz is Grateful

I recently had the good fortune to meet Henry Winkler, The Fonz, from the classic TV series *Happy Days*. There was a long line of people waiting to meet him, and he amazed me at one point with what he did. He took a break or two from taking photos with fans or signing photos for them and walked back in the line of those waiting fans to shake hands and thank the fans for taking the time to wait. He thanked them for waiting! How many celebrities do that? In a recent interview with Jaya Saxena he said he tries to keep a positive attitude and "I am just grateful" (Jaya Saxena, GQ, 5-11-2018). The Bible teaches gratitude too. Ephesians 5:20 says, "giving thanks always." An attitude of gratitude is wonderful to see expressed on the faces of people. It is refreshing. When we are waiting on the treasures of darkness to happen in our lives, to "come forth" if you will, a positive and grateful attitude goes a long way in making the wait more enjoyable.

Following Moses

Joshua 1:9 (KJV):
⁹ Have not I commanded thee? Be strong and of a good courage; be not afraid, neither be thou dismayed: for the Lord thy God is with thee whithersoever thou goest.

In Joshua chapter one, Joshua was given the daunting task of taking over for Moses. Moses had died, and it fell into Joshua's lap to lead the people into the promised land, the land flowing with milk and honey. How would you like to follow Moses? He's the one that met God in the burning bush, was given the Ten Commandments, and was such a legend that a movie was made about him and the Ten Commandments, starring Charlton Heston!

Yet God did not call Joshua to be the "second Moses" but the "first Joshua." Have you ever been in someone's shadow? In most of the cases when I followed a pastor, either the church had the previous pastor for a brief period of time or he wasn't well thought of for whatever reason. I remember once when I first came to a church to pastor and the previous pastor had only been there one year. But a lady in the church used to attend another church and would often compare me to her former pastor. He did things "this way" or "that way." You get the idea. When we face such situations, we must remember that God didn't create us to be the "second Moses."

I learned a long time ago that I can't be a copy of anyone. Even my twin brother and I, despite our similarities, differ in some ways when it comes to things we enjoy or our viewpoints. And that brings interesting aspects to a relationship. I have to be me, the personality God created in me, and so do you. I have learned when people expect me to be a carbon copy of someone else that if I truly am myself, God will bring good out of it, and someone will appreciate the real me. I have even been told that I brought new things to a church, and that is a compliment. Has that ever happened to you? Just remember—you are an original, and the artist is God.

God Never Runs Out of Blessings!

Psalm 27:13-14 (KJV):

¹³ I had fainted, unless I had believed to see the goodness of the Lord in the land of the living.

¹⁴ Wait on the Lord: be of good courage, and he shall strengthen thine heart: wait, I say, on the Lord

I remember working full-time as an inspector of small vials of medicine at a local warehouse when I was pastoring a small church in 2017. I was also writing part-time, and the combined duties of pastoring, working as an inspector, and writing became overwhelming—especially when I had to go on mandatory overtime in the inspecting job. It began to get to me. I was going to bed late and getting up early and literally had no social life. Eventually, I moved on from the inspector's job, and it led me to a treasure in the darkness. I landed a part-time job as a job coach, coaching developmentally challenged people in various jobs, such as a custodian named Randy and a dishwasher/busboy named Marc. I came to treasure my time spent with them and their personalities. They just needed friendly reminders to stay on task with their duties. This job coaching position never would have occurred had I not moved on from the inspecting job. God never runs out of blessings!

The Waiting Game

"The waiting game"—we have all played it. We have waited on a door to open regarding a job or entrance into a college or for a test result or perhaps for a medical exam's results. Or for a girlfriend to respond to the question, "Will you marry me?"

Some of the most difficult times in my life have involved waiting. I have been on unemployment a few times, and as it was nearing the end, I needed to land a job. Just before I accepted a teaching job many years ago, the insurance job I was holding came to an end. I was able to make the transition from one job to another just in the nick of time. My wife recently was laid off from her job after eighteen years, and she landed another job during the last two weeks before her unemployment compensation ended.

God has a way of making a bridge for us. He connects the dots. We sometimes wait, but then He opens the door. I remember a season in my life when I was trying to find the next church that I would pastor. There was a time when I was the candidate at one church and realized it was not a match. I waited and I waited, and the weeks passed by. I became desperate and prayed to God to please open the right door. The next day, I received three phone calls, all about open churches. I wound up going to a church in Greenville, Michigan, and pastored there for several years. The

The Treasures of Darkness

waiting game can be difficult. But God is always waiting for us when we need Him the most. And God comes through. We may feel as if we are alone in the darkness when we go through a season of waiting. But God will bring forth treasures out of that time and present us with the exact right opportunity.

Silence

At the finish of the Old Testament book of Malachi, the people of Israel were back again in Palestine following Babylonian captivity. Some 400 years passed between Malachi and the New Testament book of St. Matthew. During those 400 years, God gave the people no new word.

Have you noticed times in your life in which God has seemingly been silent? You pray and pray for answers to certain needs or simply for guidance, and the answer, it seems, is denied. The prayer for a better-paying job so you can more adequately care for your family seems to be of no avail.

At one time in my ministry, between churches, the only job I could find was working at a call center at a local Grand Rapids bank. I dealt with rude customers at times, some who cursed at me and used profanity because they were unhappy with the bank. I couldn't understand why God had placed me there. I prayed for months, and still no alternative job opened up. There were times I liked the job okay, and at other times, I could not wait for my shift to end. Have you ever been there? Yet God promises treasures shall come forth out of our dark places.

The Treasures of Darkness

    As previously stated, on two different occasions, I had the opportunity to minister to callers who were so depressed that they were contemplating suicide. I was the only agent to have gotten those types of calls. I felt like, at least during those times, I was an instrument of the Lord to encourage those two people to talk with someone and to not end their lives. Sometimes you find yourself in a tough position, but it's for a reason!

    If you are going through a protracted trial or test and it seems like you are stuck in it, even trapped, look for the treasure in the darkness. What is God bringing from it? You might have to search hard, but you should be able to come up with some treasures in the dark places. Remember, delays are not denials. God will eventually answer, and the silence will end.

Our Weakness and God's Strength

Paul wrote in 2 Corinthians 12:10: "That is why, for Christ's sake, I delight in weaknesses, in insults, in hardships, in persecutions, in difficulties. For when I am weak, then I am strong" (NIV).

My brother was diagnosed in 2014 with Parkinson's disease. He and I wept together on the phone when he told me. Before he retired a few years ago, as a pastor, he would speak in front of people, and he had already begun struggling with various symptoms from the disease. Since that first day that he told me, he suffered with his voice trembling at times while preaching, losing his balance while walking, not to mention finding it difficult to write out his sermons (he didn't type them), and with hand and leg tremors. Yet one day, he amazed me while speaking with me on the phone. He said, "I asked myself when I found out I had this disease, 'Why me?' But then I thought, 'Why not me?' I'm not exempt from suffering or going through hard times in this life." His positive attitude blessed me and reminded me of the grace God can give in this situation. He has grown even closer to his wife, Doreen, and he treasures the good days that he has. Truly, this is another example of God bringing forth treasures from the darkness. And he still manages to write in a daily journal about the goodness of the Lord. For when he is weak, he knows that because of Christ-he is strong.

The Journal

Recently, I discovered a journal that I started back in 1996. My son was three years old, just short of four, and I was working as both an instructor at the now-defunct ITT Technical Institute as well as pastoring a small church. I wrote a lot about my delight in being a father of a mischievous but cute three-year-old son, my son Daniel.

Fast forward over twenty years. It is 2017, and I rediscovered the journal in my basement. I had gotten sidetracked (for twenty years!) and the journal had been put away, possibly never to be remembered again. But as I re-read my one and only journal entry, I became intrigued with the idea of updating it. And so I did. I wrote an entry over twenty years later. My son had gotten married just a few weeks before and no longer lived at home. He had moved just weeks before from Grand Rapids to Kalamazoo. I wrote about how he still makes me laugh to this day with his quick wit and humor. I also wrote about his new wife, Kristen, and how they are devoted to one another, much like my wife Jackie and I are devoted to each other. I wrote about his love of video games and his desire to one day do commentary for video games on YouTube.

In addition, I wrote about my life now, how I am pastoring a church in Whitneyville and how my son and I recently worked together at the same company. A few years ago, we worked together at World Mission, a world-wide ministry known for sending the *Treasure*, an audio Bible, into other countries.

I read both journal entries to my son, the one from twenty years ago and the recent one. He got a kick out of it. I was amazed at the difference twenty years has made. And yet, God has remained faithful. My wife and I had a lot of financial responsibility for his wedding—paying for a nice rehearsal dinner, giving my son and daughter-in-law a nice gift, and taking care of providing a new bed (the old one was in bad condition) for my visiting brother and his wife as he was going to perform the wedding ceremony. I received a bonus check at work, unexpectedly, just before the wedding, and it helped tremendously. A treasure I re-discovered is that God was faithful twenty years ago, and He remains so yet today.

The Celebration of Life!

Nine years ago—on August 17, 2010, (it is 2019 as I write this)—I awoke with pain shooting through my shoulders. It got worse. I took an acid reducer and went back to bed. It worsened yet again. I got up, and as the pain kept increasing, I realized I was probably having a heart attack. I woke up my wife by leaning against the door frame and told her, "Honey, I think I am having a heart attack." She literally threw off the covers and leapt to her feet. I dressed and went downstairs, waiting for her to drive me to the hospital. Then I got sick and vomited in the bathroom. I had read that pain in the shoulders or jaw and vomiting were signs of a heart attack. After the vomiting, I was convinced I was having one.

We arrived in just a few minutes (I think Jackie broke the speed limit) to the hospital, St. Mary's Hospital in Grand Rapids. I walked in under my own power. But they soon got me to a room and began giving me nitro pills, then a nitro patch, and finally a nitro drip before my pain eased up a bit. The doctor confirmed I was in the middle of having a heart attack. Later that day, my heart doctor, Dr. Foster, attempted to put a stent in my heart's artery but found another blockage behind the one I had and said I would have to be transferred to another hospital in Grand Rapids for him to do it. While pulling a sheath out of my groin where they had gone through for the stent, I began to bleed and badly. I looked at a monitor and saw my heart rate go down to thirty-seven beats per minute. I heard panic in Dr. Foster's voice as he yelled to three orderlies, "Get over here and push!" They pushed on my groin area. I silently prayed, "Please God, don't let me die." I thought of my lovely wife Jackie and my seventeen-year-old son Daniel. They needed me. I was nauseated. But as they pushed, my heart rate began to climb again, and I heard the doctor say, "All right. He has color again."

I almost died twice that day. The doctor later told me that I had a 100 percent blockage in my artery, known as the "widow maker." He could not fathom why I had not died. When my wife told him I had been running on a beach in Traverse City along with my son a couple of weeks before, he had a difficult time believing it, but it was true. The Bible tells us in Hebrews 9:27 that it is appointed unto men once to die, and then after that the judgment. I know in my heart that no one is going to die until it is the "appointment" time! I am proof of that.

Dr. Foster was able to put two stents in for me, and he scheduled me for a third one. I had a 70 percent blockage in that artery, and he didn't want to let that go. Yet when I went in about a week later for that surgery, it had opened up and now was about a 40 percent blockage! The doctor didn't need to put the third stent in. He and the nurse stated they had never seen anything like that happen before. My sister-in-law Debbie put in a word for the Lord when she said, "He's a minister—you know that, right?"

A year later, on August 17, 2011, my wife Jackie wanted to celebrate my still being alive, and so we celebrated at our church with fellowship and food, and she dubbed the day, "The Celebration of Life Day." We have celebrated every year since 2011. Just a while ago, she and I went out to a nice dinner and celebrated seven years of my life and her life since that day.

I thought about all that has happened since seven years ago. My son graduated in May 2012, and I would have missed that. My son just got married two years ago on July 15, 2017, to a wonderful girl named Kristen, and I would have missed that too. I am pastoring a new church in Whitneyville—Whitneyville Fellowship Church—and I would have missed that too. I would have missed making new friends, and I would even have missed the new *Star Wars* movies! And I would have missed seeing my twin brother Bill celebrate twenty-five years as pastor of Faith Temple Church in Brighton, Michigan. God has been good. Jackie dubbed it right—it is a celebration of life. God gave me treasures in my darkness.

Frustrations but Renewals

God truly works all things together for good. His Word says in Romans 8:28: "And we know that in all things God works for the good of those who love him, who have been called according to his purpose" (NIV).

After I moved on from pastoring a church in Reed City in 2012, I had to take two difficult jobs in order to simply survive and pay the bills. I worked at a bank in customer service, taking calls and helping customers with their banking needs and with issues such as late fees. Anyone that ever has worked in customer service knows it is not an easy job. I had to deal with angry and, at times, hostile customers. I had people that hung up on me. I had to remember that it was the bank they thought of when talking to me, not Edwin Carpenter.

Yet on two occasions, I had customers call that had late fees, and both of the ladies were so distraught over their finances and their difficult situations that they mentioned suicide. I encouraged both of them to talk to someone or get to a church, and I believe I helped both of them. No one else I spoke with at the bank received a call like that. I took comfort in knowing that I was God's messenger of comfort to those two ladies at that time.

The other job I moved on to was in a factory, working on product lines in addition to skid loading. I had very little factory experience and no skid loading experience to speak of. There were days I literally lifted some 400 boxes or more. Some of the product lines moved very fast, and when I first started the job, I would become frustrated trying to keep up.

In addition, I had too many would-be bosses. One person would tell me how they thought I should do a job, and someone else would come along and tell me a totally different way to do it! On one product line, I had to walk fast, going from one end of the line to the other to take care of two different jobs. One of the jobs was to provide boxes of tubes to a person to place on the line. I literally had over ten people tell me in a short time as they walked by to not forget to move fast and to remember the tubes at the other end. After hearing it over and over, I admit it started getting to me. I remember grabbing a box that needed to be torn down, ripping it with all my might, and thrusting it into a bin in frustration. A fellow worker saw me and asked, "Is everything all right?" But something wonderful came out of my time at this factory. I met two wonderful Christian friends, John and Amy. John, like me, has moved on from the factory, and Amy and I became coworkers again. So, despite my frustrations of working there for approximately a year and a half, I gained two great friends that attend church with Jackie and me now. Again, God brought treasures out of my dark places.

Unusual Answers

I once read an anonymous story about a woman that was in a jam. She had accidentally locked her keys in her car. There was no one around to help, and although she had attempted to use a coat hanger on her window to get the car door open, it ended up being to no avail. She stopped for a moment and prayed. She had just finished her prayer when down the road, a man rode toward her on a motorcycle. This man had unkempt hair, a growth of beard, was wearing a leather jacket, and looked a bit rough. She said aloud, "Lord, is this the answer to my prayer?" But the man stopped and offered to help, and in less than a minute, he had her car door open after using the coat hanger.

"You are such a nice man," said the woman to him.

"Lady, I really am not a nice man," he replied. "I actually just got out of prison a few hours ago."

"Oh? What for?" she asked.

"For stealing cars!" the man replied.

The lady looked to the sky and said, "Thank you, Lord, You even sent me a professional!"

This humorous story makes a point. God helps us in the time of trouble, the dark times, but He may use someone we never would have dreamed of. And we don't have to be seasoned Christians to get God's attention. The Bible says God is rich to all that call upon Him (Rom. 10:12). And remember, the Titanic was built by professionals, but an amateur named Noah built the ark! We all know that the ark survived while the Titanic did not. God can use people we would not expect.

I once had a car repair that was going to be $400. I didn't have the money to repair my car. My brother gave me a check and said someone in his church wanted to bless us. The check was for $800! It was twice the amount we needed. When I tried to guess who in his church might have helped us, one of my guesses was that it was a retired couple that had done well during their careers. My brother told me, "Ed, sometimes God uses someone you would least expect." I actually had the feeling that it might be a widow in his church. God has many sources to meet our needs. We just need to pray and leave the rest to Him. Just remember, sometimes in the dark, we have to speak this one word: "Help!"

Sympathy for Others on Their Bad Days

The Bible says in Matthew 5:41, "And whosoever shall compel thee to go a mile, go with him twain (or two)" (KJV). When people we know are going through dark and isolated places in life, "going the extra mile" can make a difference in someone else's life.

I remember working with a lady once named Jerri. She was unexpectedly fired a couple of days before Christmas. I thought that this was terrible. She had a couple of kids at home, and I personally was upset that this happened just before the holidays. My wife and I agreed to help her out, and we found a church that was willing to donate food to her while she attempted to get back on her feet. She was extremely grateful. When we go the extra mile, it often comes back our way.

A few years later, the exact same thing happened to me. A Christian company let me go a week before Christmas! I was devastated. But I asked fellow Christians to pray, and guess what happened? This time I was a recipient. Several people brought us food, and one day, we found a ham left outside our door. People were going the extra mile, just as my wife and I had done for Jerri some years earlier.

The book of James tells us it is not enough to wish someone well when they are devoid of basic needs such as food. We must help them (James 2:16). And the scripture placed in the text above from Matthew 5:41 makes it clear that if we are asked to go a mile with someone, we should go two! Go the extra mile. That is where we get that phrase.

In a simple example, I once met Mark Hamill, Luke Skywalker himself, from *Star Wars*. He was very gracious. After speaking with him just a few moments, someone else was waiting to meet him, but I had wanted a photo with him. When my wife got the camera out, Mark noticed this and leaned over in the middle of his conversation to "pose" with me. I was truly touched. He may be a powerful Jedi, but he is also a very nice man!

This may not be an example of darkness, but it is definitely an example of going the extra mile as a very busy man made my day by taking a few extra moments of his time to pose for a photo with me. And you know what? I have that photo on my wall at home to this day.

I have seen people at supermarkets help a stranded motorist and lend jumper cables to give someone's dead car battery a jump. I have seen people give rides to people who were stranded. I am sure these people who helped were busy, but they went the extra mile.

Remember, go the extra mile to help someone in their time of darkness. It may come back your way—and sooner than you think!

Jobs: The Good, the Bad, and the Ugly

One area or compartment of a person's life that can cause dissatisfaction and discouragement is the place where he/she works. Our jobs can be very fulfilling and satisfying or just the opposite—they can be a source of unhappiness and a place that one dreads to go to every day.

Here is something I came across recently that made me laugh a bit—so many of these comments are true. The piece is called "What job ads 'really' mean":

> "Competitive Salary" really means, "We remain competitive by paying you less than our competition." And "Join our fast-paced company" means, "We have no time to train you." "Some overtime required" means, "Some every night and some every weekend." "Duties will vary" means, "Anyone in the office can boss you around." And "Seeking candidates with a wide variety of experience" means, "You'll need it to replace the three people who just

quit." And "Problem-solving skills a must" means, "You're walking into perpetual chaos." "Requires team leadership skills" means, "You'll have the responsibilities of a manager, without the pay or respect." Finally, "Good communication skills" means, "Management communicates, you listen, figure out what they want and do it" (Dom Carter, Netmag, January 22, 2016, for some of them, others are anonymous).

I have, sadly, worked for a few places that were strong on the above examples! I am sure nearly everyone reading this has as well, at least at one time or another. Yet I have made friends in these places, earned money to support my family, and eventually appreciated the better job I moved on to. If you are in a valley or a dark place right now regarding your job, remember—there are at least a few things or few people to be grateful for at your job, and there is always the hope that as you apply for more suitable jobs, that call with a job offer may come when you need it the most!

Reunion: A Wonderful Word

I like the word "reunion." It conjures up images of embracing loved ones and friends we haven't seen in a long time with smiles aplenty. One of my earliest childhood memories is of a reunion with my twin brother, Bill. We couldn't have been more than four or five years old. We were not raised together due to health issues regarding both my mother and me. He lived with my mom and dad for a while in Baltimore, Maryland, and then in Oklahoma for a time.

I knew my mom was bringing him to my home, where I lived with my grandparents, on Hyne Road in Brighton, Michigan, to visit me. It was getting late, and I had just headed up to bed, disappointed he hadn't made it. Then I heard some voices downstairs and realized my brother had come in. I heard him say my name, and he repeated it a few times that he wanted to see me. He was told I was in bed, but that didn't stop him from speaking up! I remember heading downstairs with excitement and seeing him, wearing a little navy blue sailor's uniform. You know how parents dress their kids sometimes! We actually grinned at each other with shyness for a moment or two. We hadn't seen each other in a long while. But then we went to one another and hugged and started talking.

We didn't get to live together until years later when we were both fifteen. My mother moved into an apartment connected to my grandparents' home and brought Bill and my sister Loretta and younger brother Jeff. I think my oldest sister Sue had married my brother-in-law Bill Cipponeri by this time.

Bill and I got to go to high school together for a few years and hang out and socialize with our friends. It was wonderful.

One other reunion that vividly stands out in my memory is when my Uncle Elmer, who lived in the South, visited after not seeing my grandmother, his mother, for many years. He got a bus ride close to the old house on Hyne Road, but he had to walk the remaining distance. I remember seeing him on a bright, sunny day, walking down the road and heading to us. My grandmother was so excited to see him that she walked speedily, almost running, to meet him and hug him. It was a loving sight I have never forgotten.

One day, there will be a heavenly reunion in Christ, in which we will be reunited with our loved ones. My grandparents and dad have been gone for several years now. I look forward to when the Lord comes back to earth and catches us up to be with our loved ones forever (1 Thess. 4:16-18). Now that is a reunion you don't want to miss! You may miss your loved ones that have passed on, but thanks to God, we have the blessed hope of a wonderful reunion.

In a Jam but don't fear: Jesus will show up!

God is with us in a jam! I have read how He will never leave us nor forsake us (Heb. 13:5), and how His angel encamps around about those that fear the Lord, and delivers them (Ps. 34:7).

Some years back when my son Daniel was still living at home, my wife, Daniel, and I were driving down 44th Street in Wyoming, Michigan, following a nice meal at Burger King. And the transmission on my Ford Taurus died on me. We literally had to stop in the right lane of a fairly busy road. Fortunately, there was a church parking lot close to us. The problem was the driveway was on an incline, and my wife Jackie, son Daniel, and I all tried to push it up into the driveway but without success. The car was too heavy and the incline too high. All of a sudden, a man came out of nowhere that looked like Shaquille O'Neal, the famous, big, strong, and tall basketball player. I mean, this guy was *built!* He got behind the car and pushed, and it was in the church parking lot in nothing flat. I made sure the car was in park, and I turned to thank the man, but he was gone. I mean, he was literally nowhere to be seen. I looked at the busy road and didn't see him getting into a car or anything like that. Could it be he was an angel?

Hebrews 13:2 says, "Be not forgetful to entertain strangers; for thereby some have entertained angels unawares" (KJV). Could it be he was an angel dispatched to help us? All I know is we were in a jam and didn't know what to do, and he showed up just like that. If he wasn't an angel, he sure *acted* like one!

That reminds me of a story of three missionaries on a trip who had run out of money. They could not afford to purchase train tickets to continue their journey. They prayed together and got in line by faith, not knowing what better to do. Suddenly, a Hungarian woman in front of them got out of line, handed one of the missionaries her money and said something in Hungarian, and then walked away. It was just enough money for the three missionaries to purchase train tickets. One of the missionaries joked that he found out angels are Hungarian! It might have simply been a Hungarian woman, but there's no doubt that God answered their prayer. When you're in a jam, remember, the situation may be dark, but God's light is still very much with you.

Encouragement in the Darkness

Recently, I was feeling a bit down. Several things in a row had gone wrong, and doors were closing, but none were opening. We all go through times of tests and trials, and sometimes, we simply have to wait on God's timing. It is vital to have people in our lives that truly care about us. My brother, Bill, sensed on the phone that I was a bit down, and later on, he sent me this e-mail:

> Hi Ed. I know this has been a difficult time for you. But I love you and so does God. I am praying for you, and I KNOW God is going to answer! I don't want to say anything that sounds hollow or shallow. I don't pretend to know why you are going through what you are going through. But I DO know that God is FOR you and that you are going to come out of this on top. I will continue to knock on heaven's door for you. I love you brother and I believe in you. Love, Bill.

Can you see why this e-mail lifted my spirit and encouraged me? It was like water to a thirsty man in a desert! Some people are not fortunate enough to have family members who can encourage them like this. If you are one of those people, I encourage you to hang out with fellow believers and friends who *will* encourage you. Also, remember that David encouraged himself in the Lord (1 Sam. 30:6). You can do this by reading Scripture, praying, listening to uplifting music, and reminding yourself of past highlights and victories. One of the treasures that God brings out of our lives is the treasure of family and friends who stand with us.

The Treasures of Darkness: Adversity

Recently, I experienced one of the best days and worst days of my life all in the same day! On March 19, 2008, I attended the play *12 Angry Men* in Grand Rapids and met the star of the show, Richard Thomas, who also is well-known for playing John-Boy Walton on the classic TV series *The Waltons*. I grew up watching that show, and Mr. Thomas was a joy to meet. During that day before the performance that night, I learned that the non-profit organization I work for was struggling financially as donations were down. I was told that I would have to--along with other staff members-- take a 40 percent cut in pay, at least temporarily. The news was difficult to hear. No one likes to find out that he will be bringing in 40 percent less pay for his family. The ironic thing is that I was actually due for a raise that month!

Following that bad news, my computer crashed on me, and because of the cut in pay, I couldn't afford the $450 repair bill. The motherboard had bitten the dust on my PC. In addition, I had to get some work done on my car, and the dealership paid for me to rent a car. I would have to pay extra for insurance for it, but I only needed it for less than a day, and with money being tight, I opted not to purchase the insurance.

Sometime between the time I took the car and the time I returned it, apparently when it was parked at home or at work, someone hit the back bumper and left scratches on it! Can you relate to this kind of streak in your life when nothing goes right for a while?

> 2 Corinthians 4:8-9 says, "We are troubled on every side, yet not distressed; we are perplexed, but not in despair; Persecuted, but not forsaken; cast down, but not destroyed" (KJV).

Following the bad news about my computer, my supervisor loaned me an older one from work and said since I used it occasionally for my job at home, I could use it as long as I needed to. Also, I heard no more news about owing for repair work on the rental car after I advised my insurance company that I was not hit from behind while driving. I am still at a reduced wage for the time being, but God has brought some blessings to us from other sources, and we are holding our own. God can use adversity, and as we continue to trust in Him, He will make a way for things to work out. Adversity can be advantageous when we look to God. God can bring light out of the darkness.

There's Hope for this Life!

Psalm 27:13-14 offers hope for those of us who are in the shade with no light in sight.

¹³I had fainted, unless I had believed to see the goodness of the LORD in the land of the living.
¹⁴Wait on the LORD: be of good courage, and he shall strengthen thine heart: wait, I say, on the LORD."

(KJV)

I remember working full-time as an inspector of small vials of medicine at a local warehouse when I was pastoring a small church in 2017. I was also writing part-time, and the combined duties of pastoring, working as an inspector, and writing became overwhelming—especially when I had to go on mandatory overtime in the inspecting job. It began to get to me. I was going to bed late and getting up early and literally had no social life. Eventually, I moved on from the inspector's job, and it led me to a treasure in the darkness. I landed a part-time job as a job coach, coaching developmentally challenged people in various jobs, such as a custodian named Randy and a dishwasher/busboy named Marc. I came to treasure my time spent with them and their personalities. They just needed friendly reminders to stay on task with their duties. This job coaching position never would have occurred had I not moved on from the inspecting job. For a time, I was overwhelmed with overwork, but eventually I was overwhelmed with the enjoyment of my new job—another treasure that came from the darkness.

Timing is Everything

Delays—we don't like them. We are so used to instant gratification when it comes to eating, such as instant eating at drive-thru restaurants and fast-food eateries. Microwave ovens heat up TV dinners and leftovers and make popcorn in a few minutes, ready to serve. People can order Pay-per-view events instantly on their cable and satellite systems. We can instantly e-mail someone in another country and sometimes instantly receive a reply. So when it comes to prayer requests to the Lord, we sometimes become antsy if the answer isn't an instant answer. Yet as someone eloquently said, delays are not denials. God has a perfect time to answer.

David did not become king as soon as he was anointed by the prophet Samuel. Many years passed. David passed many tests and overcame serious trials. When he did begin to rule at the age of thirty, he was first ruler over the kingdom of Southern Judah and not over the entire nation of Israel, not until some years later. When it was the perfect time, the right time, then he ruled all of Israel.

So, if you are waiting on something—an answer to prayer regarding a job, a relationship, a need, or whatever the case may be—just remember that God has a right time and a perfect time.

In Psalms 5, David writes in verse 3: "In the morning I lay my requests before you, and wait in expectation." This is what we need to do. Wait in expectation. Delays are not denials. The best answer God can give will come at the best time!

Sincerity Meets Sarcasm but Keep Knocking on the Door

In Matthew chapter 7, Jesus speaks of knocking on the door until it is opened, an analogy of perseverance in prayer. As I was writing this book, I was downsized from my full-time job as an editor for The Dove Foundation to a part-time employee. I have searched hard for months and sent out more resumes than I care to remember in order to find work. The unemployment rate is currently near 10 percent in many states.

There are times in which even our sincerity is challenged. I wrote a local newspaper editor to tell him about my background and to ask about sending a resume to apply for work. This was his response: "Your timing could not be worse than if you were a guy with silent-actor skills but a squeaky voice and we were just introducing talking pictures."

This was the only response I received from him. It was a cutting response. I had written a very sincere e-mail and told him a little about my background, and then he chose to reply with a sardonic answer which lacked compassion. I wrote in return: "Then with the introduction of the talkies I would take "bit" parts and more training until my moment to shine finally arrived…"

I tried to respond with some wit and a total lack of bitterness but with a belief that my moment to shine would still arrive. If any reader of this page has traveled through a time of sincerely attempting to do something legitimate only to have sarcasm or a lack of interest thrown your way, rest assured that God still honors faith. Jesus stated that if we knock on the door, it will be answered. I have had people knock on my door, and almost everyone will rap on the door at least three or four times and then knock at least another time or two if there is not an immediate response. If I heard a single knock on my door, I would think a disoriented bird had flown into my door by accident! I have learned to keep knocking, and from past experience, the door ultimately will open. This is a treasure you can glean from difficult times. Don't give up. Face sarcasm in the face. Keep knocking!

Face the Music

In Psalms chapter 51, King David took responsibility for his sin and asked the Lord's forgiveness. David, a man after God's own heart, had had an affair with the beautiful Bathsheba. This was very un-God like. Then, to make matters worse, once he had learned she was pregnant, he sent her husband Uriah the Hittite to the forefront of a heated battle, where he was killed. However, the prophet Nathan brought the word of the Lord to him and confronted him with his wrongdoing.

David had to "face the music." Have you ever heard that phrase before? Its origins are uncertain. One school of thought says that it comes from musical theatre. A nervous or inexperienced performer would have to summon up all his courage to face the audience, which would require him also to face the musicians in the orchestra pit, a cynical and world-weary group. They have seen everything. A second possibility is that the phrase is of military origin. It could relate to a soldier taking his place in the ranks during an assembly, facing the military band. It could mean a cavalryman attempting to keep his restless horse quiet while the band plays, or it could refer to a soldier being drummed out of his regiment.

Whatever the case, most of us are familiar with this phrase. We all have to "face the music" from time to time. Recently, when daylight savings time began again, I somehow missed the news. On a Sunday morning, I was scheduled to speak at a church in Grand Ledge, Michigan. I arrived an hour late, and they had just finished the service! I felt terrible about it. I was scheduled to speak again that evening, and when I stepped up on the platform, I immediately faced the music and apologized for my mistake. I thought it was the least I could do. I joked that I had kidded other church members in the past when they showed up late after the clocks were put forward and maybe I had teased them so much that God was allowing me to go through it now!

When we sin and when we fail others, we have to face the music and admit it and take responsibility. Jim Bakker, the famous TV evangelist who used to head up the *Praise the Lord* program, had to face the music when it was learned in the late eighties that he had misappropriated funds. Yet after he paid his dues, he wrote a book titled *I Was Wrong*. He faced the music, and many people were glad he humbled himself in that way.

How about you and your situations? How about your marriage? Is it going downhill, and could it possibly be your fault? In the film *Fireproof,* Fire Chief Caleb Holt has to face the fact his marriage to Catherine is fading fast. They argue all the time. When his father gives him the book *The Love Dare*, Caleb is challenged to perform an act of kindness every day for forty days to express his love to his wife and attempt to win his love again. His heart is not in it at first, and there is no improvement in the marriage. When he finally realizes his heart hasn't been in it, he begins to sincerely express his love for Catherine. Early on, he had given her some pitiful flowers as a gift. This time, he buys her some beautiful red roses, and the viewer sees that her heart is touched. He is beginning to win her back.

Many times, we must face the music and make adjustments. If we are struggling financially, we might have to do what Dave Ramsey says and "act our wage" (*Dave Ramsey's Financial Peace University*). My wife and I prospered a lot just a few years ago, but the last year has been the opposite. We have struggled to simply pay bills and buy food. We have had to adjust our budget by facing the music and the fact that we are dealing with less income than before.

We need to do three things in order to face the music. We need to, first of all, be honest about the situation. This humorous story makes a good point about being less than honest. One day, an employee of a certain company received an unusually large check. He decided not to say anything about it. The following week, his check was for less than the normal amount, and he confronted his boss. "How come," the supervisor inquired, "you didn't say anything when you were overpaid?"

Unruffled, the employee said, "Well, I can overlook one mistake—but not two in a row!" We might laugh at this story, but it makes a point that the employee wasn't honest and didn't truly face the music.

Secondly, we need to keep our faith when facing the music. We may be going through a difficult time, but God promised to be with us always in Matthew chapter 28. When Joseph was betrayed by his brothers, he could have given up hope, but he kept doing the right things and keeping the right attitude. Eventually, he was made the prime minister of all of Egypt. After a great famine devoured the land, Joseph's brothers came to Egypt for help as they and their father Jacob were running out of food. Joseph eventually revealed himself to his brothers in the story, who didn't recognize him because a lot of years had passed and they had believed him to be dead. He went and forgave them, and they had to face the music. The very one they had betrayed now was the man who fed them and saved them.

So, we need to be honest when we face the music, we need to retain our faith, and, thirdly, we need to complete the journey. An example of this is a couple I heard about who owed thousands of dollars to credit card companies. They decided they had had enough. They quit using the cards, spent very carefully, quit eating out for a time, and even had several yard sales to raise money. In less than three years, they were out of debt. They did this by facing the music and completing the mission of their goal.

What situation are you facing today? Face the music honestly, and God will help you.

Spend Your Time Wisely

The Bible tells us to redeem the time, or to use it wisely (Eph. 5:16). Life is fleeting. The grains of sand in the overturned hourglass are falling fast. We cannot retrieve time once it has passed. God brings hidden treasures to us when we use our time wisely.

No man on a deathbed ever said he wished he had spent more time making money. However, some people on deathbeds have said they wished they had spent more time with their families or serving God or both. Notice the word just used—"spent." It means used. When you spend money, it is used up and gone. When your energy is spent, it means you are drained and you have nothing left. When time is spent, it can never be recalled.

Do at least one thing today that you know is a worthy way of spending your time. Call or visit a friend. Pray to God for a while. Volunteer to help someone out or a good cause. Read a book you have been meaning to get to. When we spend our time wisely, we nourish our own souls and, very often, touch the souls of others.

Faith Sees the Invisible

The Bible says in 1 Peter 1:8-9 that our faith is rewarded with the salvation of our souls. The King James Version says "receiving the end of your faith," which means the result or reward of our faith. I like how this is termed because faith has a beginning, when we believe, and faith has an end, when we receive. It goes well beyond salvation, and even now, I am sure that every reader of this book is facing a situation in which you need to first believe so that the end result will be a reward of your faith.

I knew a woman named Sheila who lived in Greenville, Michigan. Several years ago, a new K-mart store was about to open, and the store was flooded with applications. Sheila stated that she would land one of the jobs. She needed a job, and she stated that God would not let her down. Out of the hundreds of applications that the store received, they turned to Sheila as one of the people they hired. She had no special skills that merited her favor. God gave her the favor. Faith began when she believed there was a job with her name on it. Faith ended when she landed the job. The end result was a reward for her faith—the job she desired.

We will find treasures in dark places when we continue to believe—no matter how grey the skies or threatening, no matter how silent the heavens, no matter how barren the desert land.

Paul stated that we should "fight the good fight of faith," (1 Tim. 6:12). In Ephesians chapter 6 when Paul mentioned all the pieces of armor that we need to fight the spiritual battles, he said that above all, we should take the shield of faith (Eph. 6:16).

God has Our Number

Years ago when Jackie and I pastored in Greenville, Michigan, I worked on a budget one day and discovered we were about $45 short of being able to pay the monthly bills and buy groceries. She and I prayed together and believed that God would help close the gap of that crack in the budget. Within two days, I received a totally unexpected phone call. Wrangler Blue Jeans company was looking for someone to count blue jeans at a store not far away, and it would only take a couple of hours a month. The pay, however, would be quite good. It would pay $45—the exact amount we needed for our budget! My wife took the part-time job and enjoyed it very much, and our budget concerns were solved. To this day, I do not know how that lady got our phone number, but God had our number! He knew our needs.

We all know that God is a God of possibilities, and yet in Hebrews 11:6, the Bible says it is impossible to please God without faith. Whenever the word "impossible" is used in the same sentence with the word "God," we'd better pay attention! God says we *must* have faith. As someone wisely said, faith will not eliminate our battles, but it will carry us through to victory. Since the Bible also says it has been given to every man to have the measure of faith (Rom. 12:3), we know that we must simply use the faith we have. Are you facing a struggle? Do you have a need? First off, believe. Then, receive the end of that faith—the answer!

God Rises

Psalms 12:5 says that God rises to defend us against our enemies. In a recent survey on *Family Feud*, a TV game show, the category was "give an example of something that rises." People surveyed mentioned bread and yeast, temperatures, and the tide and people. I thought of balloons and then I thought, "God rises too." In the same verse in Psalms which we just read, it says, "I will now arise, says the Lord" (NIV). Psalms 102:13 says that God will arise and have compassion on us.

Whatever your political persuasion, I remember after 9/11 that our country was literally reeling. President George W. Bush had been our president for less than a year. He was known as a fair orator—certainly not an Abraham Lincoln, but adequate. Yet when he spoke to the nation and to both Republicans and Democrats, he said we would stand up to the enemy, and I remember he gave the best speech up to that point I had heard him give. Several times, members of both political parties rose to their feet and applauded. Even Hillary Clinton stood and cheered. The thought struck me--*He just rose to the occasion.*

Sometimes, we wait on God. We wait on His answers. But God knows when to arise and to respond, and according to Scripture, He always times it just right. Psalms 68:1 says, "Let God arise and his enemies be scattered." When Stephen was being stoned, according to the book of Acts, chapter 7:54-60, he looked up at the heavens and said he saw God sitting on His throne and Jesus standing on His right hand. Was Jesus rising to come to his rescue if it was the Father's will? Or was He simply rising to greet Stephen? We know for certain that He did rise and welcomed Stephen home when he died as a martyr. In Malachi 4:2, the Bible says that the Sun of Righteousness will arise with healing in His wings. This refers to Christ and the millennial reign. Yet as with many scriptures, the law of double reference is working in this passage. Christ also restores and rises to help His people now. When He returns, it will be a perfect resolution of all our battles and struggles, and peace will reign.

I hope as you face this day and this week you will have an image in your mind of God rising to show you favor and to reveal His compassion to you and to come to your aid. It is the perfect and completely accurate picture of our God.

Treasures Lie Below

As I write this on February 18, President's Day, it has snowed and been blustery cold. Michigan has received almost double the snow this year when compared to the same time last year. I have cleaned off my car many mornings now and shoveled the snow constantly in my driveway and off my porch. Sometimes, the word "redundant" doesn't seem to do it justice. Yet I read something the other day that I liked, a forecast of a different kind. It simply said, "Jesus reigns forever." That thought has helped me during the dead and biting times of cold, which I have experienced during the winter solstice and months of shortened days. Life can seem dull during the barren winter months, and yet there are seeds just waiting to bloom into lovely flowers in a few short months. The treasure lies beneath. When we go through those times in our lives when the routine is a bit boring, we must remember that good things lie beneath the snow and also await to spring forth in our lives in a short while. Jesus reigns forever!

Sad to Glad

The shortest verse in the Bible is John 11:35: "Jesus wept." Think about the short sentences we say, sometimes frequently in one day—"I'm angry," "I'm upset," "I can't," "Who cares?" The reason Jesus wept is because of His compassion for Lazarus, who had died, and his sisters Martha and Mary, who were in mourning. Because Jesus had compassion on us and died on the cross of Calvary and said three great words, "It is finished," meaning He completed God's plan of salvation for man, we now can utter different short sentences. We can say, "I'm coping," "It's okay," "I can," and "Jesus cares."

God gives us treasures in darkness because Jesus wept. He carried our griefs and sorrows according to Isaiah 53:4. We can turn the sentences around from "I'm sad" to "I'm glad." We can say, "I'm walking by faith," instead of, "I don't understand"— what a treasure in the darkness. Try saying these affirmation words the next time you are tempted to utter negative sentences. Because Jesus wept, we can laugh in hope.

Imitation

The Bible instructs us in Hebrews 13:7 to imitate the faith of those who are spiritual leaders. We can learn from pastors and ministers and Sunday school teachers and elders and those who have successfully lived spiritual lives and are seasoned in the Christian faith.

Recently, my family and I went to Philadelphia and Virginia on vacation. While in Philadelphia, we made a stop at the Philadelphia Museum of Art. The purpose of our visit was to run up the museum steps, just as the character Rocky did in the *Rocky* films. That day, I saw several other people who had the same dream. I remember running up a lot of steps, and it got a bit tougher as I neared the top; but hey, if Rocky did it, certainly Ed Carpenter could do it too! I made it to the top, and in my best Rocky Balboa pose, I jumped up and down with my hands lifted in victory. I really relished the moment. Why? Because Rocky overcame many obstacles in the *Rocky* films, which are very inspirational, and I had aspired to run to the top of the steps the same as he. He was a role model of sorts to me. I felt, in a small way, that I too had accomplished something significant, as Rocky before me had done.

Paul spoke to his followers to follow him as he first followed Christ. A wise man once said that imitation is the sincerest form of flattery. That is why people every day, from every walk of life, run up the museum steps in Philadelphia. They long to imitate one who has inspired them. Christ said in John 16:33 that He had overcome the world. Now He is one I want to imitate! I have learned that when I successfully imitate Him, I find some treasures in the darkness.

A Thousand Faces

The famous silent film star Lon Chaney was called, "The Man of a Thousand Faces" because he used so many different ones from his famous make-up case. Chaney was a master craftsman of make-up and played various film roles, such as Quasimodo in *The Hunchback of Notre Dame* and the disfigured Erik in *Phantom of the Opera*.

There are times that we display different kinds of faces, depending on our moods. We sometimes are happy and pleasant, at other times moody and angry, and at other times even difficult or short with others. Consistency is an important quality that we should strive for. If you have ever known someone who is the same every time you see them and, conversely, someone who is so unpredictable that you don't know which side of his or her personality will show up, then you understand the need for consistency. In this case, when we deal with people who are not consistent in their behavior or attitudes, we can bring treasure out of those dark situations by focusing on being consistent in our own daily lives. We can learn from other people's shortcomings by our own exemplary example of consistency.

Don't you appreciate consistency? The reason you attend certain restaurants regularly is because of the consistency of their service and food. My wife Jackie and son Daniel and I love a restaurant named Hunan because they are consistent in their offering of great Chinese recipes. I appreciate the promptness of my paper girl. She is consistent. We appreciate our mailman being consistent and our employer every payday.

The thousand faces worked well for Lon Chaney, and he built an entire career based on his skill with make-up and his acting abilities. But when it comes to demonstrating our Christian patience and attitude, we need to strive for one face, the face of consistency. This will result in treasures from the darkness.

Time Brings Change

Recently, I discovered a journal that I started back in 1996. My son was three years old, just short of four, and I was working as both an instructor at the now-defunct ITT Technical Institute as well as pastoring a small church. I wrote a lot about my delight in being a father of a mischievous but cute three-year-old son, my son Daniel.

Fast forward over twenty years. It is 2017, and I rediscovered the journal in my basement. I had gotten sidetracked (for twenty years!), and the journal had been put away, possibly never to be remembered again. But as I re-read my one and only journal entry, I became intrigued with the idea of updating it. And so I did. I wrote an entry over twenty years later. My son had gotten married just a few weeks before and no longer lived at home. He had moved just weeks before from Grand Rapids to Kalamazoo. I wrote about how he still makes me laugh to this day with his quick wit and humor. I also wrote about his new wife, Kristen, and how they are devoted to one another, much like my wife Jackie and I are devoted to each other. I wrote about his love of video games and his desire to one day do commentary for video games on YouTube.

In addition, I wrote about my life now, how I am pastoring a church in Whitneyville and how my son and I recently worked together at the same company. A few years ago, we worked together at World Mission, a world-wide ministry known for sending the *Treasure*, an audio Bible, into other countries.

I read both journal entries to my son, the one from twenty years ago and the recent one. He got a kick out of it. I was amazed at the difference twenty years has made. And yet, God has remained faithful. My wife and I had a lot of financial responsibility for his wedding—paying for a nice rehearsal dinner, giving my son and daughter-in-law a nice gift, and taking care of providing a new bed (the old one was old) for my visiting brother and his wife as he was going to perform the wedding ceremony. I received a bonus check at work, unexpectedly, just before the wedding, and it helped tremendously. A treasure I re-discovered is that God was faithful twenty years ago, and He remains so yet today.

Dreams Can Come True

Be on the lookout! One definite method which works in finding treasures in darkness is to be vigilant and watchful. Years ago as a twelve-year-old boy, I enjoyed watching the family TV series *The Waltons*. In fact, when I watched a character on the show, the young man named John-Boy Walton (Richard Thomas), write down his thoughts on paper and declare he wanted to be a writer, he inspired me to begin writing for the first time. I somehow connected with Mr. Thomas's portrayal of the young writer. I began writing down my thoughts on paper and even poems and short stories.

Fast forward several years. In the summer of 2006, I saw that the Hallmark Channel was airing a family TV movie titled *Wild Hearts*. Richard Thomas was starring in it. I was the new assistant editor at The Dove Foundation, which promotes and encourages family and wholesome entertainment. I had been writing film and DVD reviews and conducting interviews with people in the motion picture and TV business. When I saw the advertisement for *Wild Hearts,* I suddenly remembered that I had a contact number of a lady who worked for the Hallmark Channel. Suddenly in that moment, I realized I might possibly be able to set up a phone interview with Richard Thomas.

In fact, the Hallmark Channel representative, a lady named Sheri, did indeed help me out, and a couple of weeks later, I interviewed Richard Thomas on the phone and then wrote up the interview, and we posted it on our website.

Imagine that—the same actor who had inspired me to take up writing gave me an interview, and I was the writer who wrote the interview with him! It felt surreal. There was certainly a feeling of having gone full circle. He gave me a wonderful interview too and was very gracious. He said he had a concern that "family programming is becoming an endangered species."

So, what is your dream? What do you hope to accomplish in life which you have not yet achieved at this point?

Be on the lookout. I believe people sometimes miss the open door of opportunity when it is staring them right in the face. Put on that thinking cap, and when your moment comes, you will be ready for it!

Good Intentions

Why is it that sometimes we get into hot water when we had good intentions? Recently, the Shout! Factory released the first season of an old TV series on DVD—*Dennis the Menace,* starring Jay North. I remembered watching the series as a kid, and I had enjoyed it, so I picked up the set. Dennis always manages to bother poor old Mr. Wilson, his retired neighbor, even though he doesn't mean to. In one episode, I watched the young boy, probably eight or nine years old, offer to help move some dirt in the wheelbarrow as Mr. Wilson is planting a small garden. He moves it *behind* Mr. Wilson, but then he has to leave suddenly, so he runs off. Mr. Wilson stands up and steps back into the wheelbarrow and falls down, knocking all the dirt out of the cart! Dennis didn't really help him after all, but he sure meant well.

When the good intentions you have don't pan out, just remember to search for the treasures in the darkness. Perhaps like this TV viewer, your good intentions will give someone a chuckle, like Dennis did for me when he meant to help Mr. Wilson. I once tried to teach myself a few things on the computer, which made a fellow instructor of mine and computer expert named Pat laugh. "I know why God put you on earth, Ed," Pat told me. "It was to amuse people like me!"

Second Chances

Nine years ago I suffered a light heart attack. At age fifty, I really didn't see such an event occurring in my life. The fact that my twin brother had stents inserted to open up the flow of blood through his arteries should have prepared me for the possibility. He had surgery in March 2010, and on Tuesday, August 17, 2010, I awoke with achy shoulders and pressure in my chest. I assumed it was acid reflux and took some medicine accordingly. However, when the ache and pressure intensified, I knew something wasn't right. I awoke my wife Jackie, and she immediately rushed me to a local hospital, St. Mary's Hospital, in Grand Rapids.

I was given three nitroglycerine pills in a row, five minutes apart; plus a nitro patch was placed on me and then a steady drip of the nitro. Finally, the pain eased from an eight on a one-to-ten scale to a two. Later, I learned that my main artery was 100 percent blocked. Little did I know a small artery behind it was also 100 percent blocked, and I had a 70 percent block in another artery. I was told it was amazing I was walking around and alive! I was scheduled to be transferred to Spectrum Health Hospital the next day and to have at least one to two stents inserted to open up the blockages. I was also told if it wasn't possible to receive the stents due to hardened blockages, I would be looking at heart bypass surgery—not the kind of news I wanted to hear. However, a first attempt was made on that Tuesday at St. Mary's Hospital. They learned more about the blockages after going up my groin with a heart catherization procedure and then ran into another problem. When they tried to remove a sheath from the groin too soon, I began to hemorrhage, and three panicky orderlies ran over to apply pressure on my groin to get the bleeding to stop. I was in danger of bleeding to death. My heart rate fell on the monitor down to thirty-seven beats per minute, and I remember thinking, *Please, God, I don't want to die like this.* At the same time, I felt at peace about the situation. Soon, I began to feel as if I were going to throw up, the worst possible thing that I could do with them working on me to stop the bleeding, but a nurse quickly gave me some medicine, which eased my nausea.

Soon, thankfully, my heart rate began to climb, and a few minutes later, I heard the surgeon, Dr. Foster, say, "He has some color again!" Some might read this and ask, "How in the world could God bring good from you having a light heart attack?" But He did! He brought treasures out of the darkness.

The next day, they successfully placed two stents in the arteries, which meant bypass surgery would not be necessary. I was relieved, to say the least. Then, they scheduled me to have a final stent put in about a week later, nine days later to be exact. When I went in on that Friday to have it done, I was still awake when I heard the surgeon, Dr. Foster, say, "This is amazing. The blockage has opened up! Ten days ago it was 70 percent blocked, and now it is only 40 percent blocked. You won't need a stent! And you will be able to go home this evening!" That was glorious news to my ears. A nurse later told me in all the years she had been in health care, she had never seen a blockage open up like that. I called it a "God" thing!

Since I was released from the hospital, I have a new sense of appreciation for the gift of life, and for the first time in a long time, I am eating healthy. I have lost around eighteen pounds and plan to continue to eat healthy. Too many trips to McDonald's and Burger King contributed to this. Moderation is the theme for me now. I am soon to start exercising and plan to do it regularly. Again, before this happened to me, I was inconsistent with exercise. So, God has brought good out of the bad, not to mention the fact that I was literally overwhelmed with get well cards, phone calls, and e-mail messages. I felt a love and support from the church I pastor, which truly amazed me and blessed me. On top of that, I have found an even closer relationship with my dear wife Jackie and son Daniel, and we were close already. Life is good, and God brings treasures out of the darkness!

Now would be Good, Lord!

Sometimes, we need to come right to the point. In Psalms 18, David praised the Lord for delivering him from the hand of Saul and from all his enemies. In verse 6, he says, "In my distress I called to the Lord; I cried to my God for help. From his temple he heard my voice; my cry came before him, into his ears." David writes in verse 9, "He parted the heavens and came down: dark clouds were under his feet."

In other words, God answered *immediately*. There are times when we wait on God to answer a prayer, but when it is an *urgent* prayer, rest assured that God can move speedily to our rescue and, in fact, *will!*

In St. Matthew chapter 14, Jesus appeared to the disciples during a storm, walking to them on the water. The disciples were frightened. Think about it. They were tired from rowing the little boat; it was late, between 3:00 and 6:00 am, plus the terrible storm no doubt frightened them. Then suddenly, they saw a figure walking upon the water. At this time in history, there was a legend about ghosts appearing during storms. Jesus assured them that it was He who was walking to them. Peter said in verse 28 that if it was indeed Jesus, to allow him (Peter) to walk on the water. Jesus said, "Come," (verse 29).

Peter started out walking, but when he saw the waves being tossed to and fro and heard the boisterous (loud) winds, he became frightened and began to sink. Friends, Peter did not have time for a long eloquent prayer at this point. There was no time to pray, "Dear Heavenly Father, I find myself in a precarious situation. Would you be so kind as to come to my rescue and help me?" No! He prayed, "Help!" His prayer was short and to the point, "Lord, save me!" At times a simple and short prayer is adequate and catches God's attention, who is always aware of where we are and what we are facing in life.

Common Sense

"If any of you lacks wisdom, he should ask God,
who gives generously to all without finding fault,
and it will be given to him" (James 1:5).

Over the years, I have experienced some of the best times of my life in church or in fellowshipping with other Christians. In fact, the word "fellowship" really means a few fellows in the same ship together. We really do need close friends in our boats with us, don't we?

At the same time, I have come across some people, and not just in the Christian community, that don't practice good common sense. Every reader of this book can probably name at least one person they know who is a sharp individual and knowledgeable when it comes to certain topics but simply does not know how to act around other people.

My wife used to be a worship leader, and everyone loved her and the job she did. For some reason, once when a couple visited us and we told them she was stepping down due to her pregnancy, the woman replied, "Oh, that's wonderful. I have been praying you would step down!" My wife was, honestly, a bit hurt, and then the woman acted totally surprised that this comment hurt her feelings, and then she wanted to hug Jackie! Duh?!

A dear lady who was in our church in Wayland had a teen daughter, and she commented to me that she often went up to her bedroom with her boyfriend but said, "Nothing happens. I know my daughter." Duh?! Two young teenagers who are crazy about each other and each with raging hormones, and nothing is going to happen if left alone in a bedroom? I should have said something, but I didn't. I minded my own business, but I thought, *How can you actually believe nothing will happen?* Sure enough, a few months later, the mother told me her daughter was pregnant. The couple eventually married, but they had placed the cart before the horse. The book of Proverbs is a book of wisdom (Proverbs 4:7), and I encourage people to read it to gain wisdom and to pray for wisdom as the book of James instructs us to do in James 1:5. If so, you will save yourself and others from embarrassment or worse, and this will enable you to find more treasures in the dark places. For example, my father once went to check on my brother Bill who was playing outside when he was a kid, and he had been alone and near a lake for a short while. My brother had walked off into the lake and stepped off into a hole and was near drowning when my dad ran to him and rescued him. Dad used common sense and checked on my brother. Thank God that he did.

My mother once checked on him too (my brother needed to be checked on a lot back then) and found he was playing with matches under the porch with my cousin Mitch. His pant leg had caught on fire, and my mother immediately patted out the fire with her hands and kept him from being badly burned. Thank God my mother used some common sense and checked on her son. I have seen kids, two years old, all by themselves and playing near busy city streets in Grand Rapids outside of their houses, and I have often thought, *Where is the parent? This precious gift of God could be taken away by an evil person, or the child could wander into the street and be hit by a car.* Common sense is needed and will provide protection for our loved ones, and God will bring treasures out of dark places. For even in our dark places, are not the people we love the greatest treasures in our life?

That Hurts!

"Ouch! That hurts." Maybe you used that expression as a child, possibly after being stung by a bee after running across lush, green grass under the sun's rays on a lazy summer day. Or possibly, the words flew from your mouth after hearing what a friend or co-worker said about you now that you are all grown up. Words can bless, and words can injure.

Most people are at least a little sensitive about something. Some people cringe if you mention their weight or their new haircut or hairstyle in an unflattering way. Others are easily wounded if something is said about one of their kids. Still others are hurt if it begins to appear that a promise made is not going to be kept. Husbands hurt wives' feelings, wives hurt husbands, children hurt parents, and for many, when a fellow Christian hurts them, it is the absolute worst kind of hurt of all.

So be it personal appearance, our family (blood is thicker than water, they say), or broken promises, we tend to get our feelings hurt and sometimes, probably too often, very easily.

I once had my feelings hurt over a trifle but managed to move on. I was the pitcher for our church softball team when I pastored in Greenville, Michigan. During a game, one of the first batters hit a lazy pop-up to me, and I had to step back about one step to get under it. I was set to catch it when our third baseman, who was far too zealous or over-anxious, raced over to get it and knocked me over. I landed hard on my wrist and broke it. I had to have pins inserted into my hand and arm with a bar placed on top to keep my wrist straight until it healed. I endured some nine weeks of this, with my faithful wife Jackie attending to the wounds around the pins and cleaning them every single day.

After the pins were removed, I had a fierce red-looking scar on my hand. This was in 1992, and the scar has faded a lot over the years, but back then, it was a nasty red. I went to shake a woman's hand in the church one Sunday morning, and I knew this young woman well. When she saw my scar, she pulled her hand back, as if I were contagious. She refused to shake my hand.

That moment must have been imprinted on my brain because I remember going over to a lady named Patty at our church in Wayland, Michigan, several years after the handshaking incident. I was going to shake Patty's hand, and just as I spoke her name, she let out a mighty sneeze on the top of her right hand, and immediately, she turned to me and put out that same hand for me to shake. Maybe I remembered in my subconscious the way I felt when my handshake had been refused. Despite the sneeze she had just placed upon her hand, I extended my hand and shook it. Now, I am not saying everyone has to react how I did. Some people would have said, "Uh, excuse me, after you take a quick trip to the ladies' room and wash that hand, I will be glad to shake it."

In my case, I remembered what it felt like to be treated like a leper, and I didn't want Patty to experience that same feeling, even though I did have cause to have waited until later to shake her hand. After all, a scar just looks bad but a fresh sneeze—that's nasty! Still, even though my son Daniel said, "Dad, I don't know how you did that! That was nasty!" I managed to do it anyways. Sometimes when we have been hurt, we want to spare others the same feelings we experienced.

In the Bible in 1 Samuel chapter 1, a woman mocked Hannah when she couldn't have children. Hannah loved her husband Elkanah but was miserable. She wanted to have his children. Still, she went to the temple to pray about it. The high priest, Eli, saw her, and she was moving her mouth as she prayed, but no words were heard. He thought she was drunk at first and scolded her. She told him she was not drunk, only praying. He encouraged her that the Lord would grant her request, and sure enough, some nine months later, she gave birth to a son and named him Samuel, meaning "asked of the Lord." Hannah took those hurt feelings and prayed about it, and God gave her a boy!

Jesus knew the sting of being hurt. His own disciple, Judas Iscariot, betrayed him. Yet Jesus called him "friend," even after Judas showed up with the soldiers who would take Him away. Judas might not have been Jesus's true friend, but Jesus sure remained his friend.

What treasures can you pull out of the darkness today? If you have been hurt and find yourself in the position of having the opportunity to hurt someone yourself, bless them instead and remember the feelings you experienced. And if you have been recently hurt, pray to the Lord as Hannah did. God can turn it around! Remember to forgive as Christ has forgiven you.

Forgetfulness can be Good

Forgetfulness isn't always bad. Recently, I spoke with my sixty-nine-year-old mother by phone, and she told me she was becoming forgetful. I tried to cheer her up and said, "Well, think about it, Mom—there are some things you probably have forgotten which you were better off not remembering!" The trick worked, and she laughed heartily. Yet isn't it true?

If someone has hurt you in the past or you were overlooked for a promotion at work or you had a day in which nothing went right, isn't it a good thing to purposely choose to forget those things? Paul wrote about this in the book of Philippians chapter 3 verse 13, when he said, "Forgetting those things which are behind…"

We can't change the past, but we can ruin today by focusing on past failures and bad days. The next time you are confronted with a bad memory from the past, pull out a treasure of darkness and remember something good that happened to you, a blessing. Remember sharing lunch with an old friend or a joke you heard that made you laugh or a day at a sporting event in which *your* team won or a day in which you got to pick up something you had wanted to buy for a long time. *Forget* the bad stuff. Remember, forgetfulness isn't always bad.

Perseverance Pays

The Frederik Meijer Gardens and Sculptures in Grand Rapids, Michigan, are housed in a beautiful place to visit. Mr. Meijer has given us a lovely place where one can enjoy nature and also look on wonderful sculptures, some of the best in the world, produced by talented artists. God sculpts our lives by our experiences and the people we know.

Abraham Lincoln ran for and lost several political offices before winning the biggest race of all, the office of president of the United States of America. His hardships, being raised as a rail splitter in Kentucky and suffering bankruptcy and then cutting his political teeth by losing several races, sculpted him into the man who became a father of this nation and helped to heal this country during and after the Civil War.

Frank Herbert tried selling his science fiction novel *Dune* to twenty publishers and was turned down twenty times. He sent the book to the twenty-first publisher, who published his book, and it became a best-selling book.

The same sun that hardens clay softens wax. It is up to us to remain pliable and to learn and grow and allow God to sculpt our

Perseverance Pays

lives. A lot of work went into the sculptures in Meijer Gardens. Only the finished product is seen. A lot of people have never seen what we have endured to get to the place where we are today. They only see what we have become—a lawyer, teacher, factory worker, parent, musician, or writer. And yet with each vocation just listed, a tremendous amount of work, education, and practice goes into accomplishing our best in these positions. Life tends to sculpt us, and we become the people we are.

Let's determine to always remain curious, pliable, and willing to learn new things. Many senior citizens have become proficient at using computers and even running and maintaining their own websites. They have continued to learn and be sculpted. We are not finished sculptures, but we can get closer and closer to perfection if we remain like clay in the Potter's hands.

Humility Helps

Sometimes employees can offer sound advice to an employer. Such was the case when Naaman, captain of the host of the king of Syria, was instructed by the prophet Elisha to dip himself in the Jordan River seven times to be cleansed of his leprosy (2 Kings 5:10).

Naaman stubbornly refused. He wanted the man of God to come wave his hand over the place like a magician, and then he would be healed. He, in effect, wanted the townsfolk to see a great show, with himself as the main attraction.

Naaman also resented the idea of ducking in the dirty Jordan River. He even stated that the rivers of Damascus were better than all the waters of Israel (2 Kings 5:12).

His servants came full focus into the picture at this point. They pointed out that he would obey if he could do some great thing but how much better it would be to listen to Elisha and be cleansed. Simple but sound advice in one word—obey.

The prophet Samuel told Saul that obedience is better than sacrifice and to hearken is better than the fat of rams (1 Sam. 15:22).

Naaman finally listened and ducked himself in the Jordan River. But he wasn't cleansed until he went under the seventh time. Only complete obedience will bring the full blessings of God into one's life.

When Jesus performed His first miracle at the marriage feast in Cana, it took faith on behalf of the servants. He instructed them to fill the six large water pots with water. They wanted wine, not water. Yet Mary had told them, "Do whatever he tells you" (John 2:5).

What instruction in one sentence! Whatever the Lord tells you to do, do it. The servants obeyed. When they drew from the water to present it to the governor of the feast, it had turned into wine.

The Lord's instructions are not always easy to follow, but if we obey in the dark, we shall see the light.

In His word, the Lord gives us instructions which don't always make sense to the natural man — give to receive, humble yourself to be exalted, and be last to be first. However, these instructions work.

Naaman learned this when he was cleansed after seven ducks in dirty water. The Lord's ways may be mysterious, but they are also marvelous.

Common Ground

I once heard a great line from, of all places, an old TV western called *Have Gun-Will Travel*.

The character of Paladin was speaking about romance and said, "Common sense never did much good after meeting Cupid" (*Have Gun-Will Travel, CBS Television*). How true! People too often let their hearts rule their heads. I claim to be no expert regarding issues of the heart, but it seems to me that marriages last much longer (as they should) when two people have at least a few of the same interests. Some couples enjoy collecting antiques together, playing golf or bowling, or traveling. I have met couples who had nothing in common, and the only reason they seemed to be together was that one partner was male and the other was female! If you are in a relationship, even if you have to develop an interest in something your partner likes or if you can come up with something you both enjoy, the chances of your marriage lasting grows immensely.

The Bible says in 1 Corinthians 13:8 that love never fails. Give your prospective marriage or your current relationship a real chance. Find a hobby or two that you and your partner can love together. You will discover treasures out of darkness.

Attitude, Attitude!

Have you ever had a really bad teacher—a teacher who wasn't patient or didn't seem to genuinely care or was not interested in taking time out of class to help you? Have you ever had a boss who was uncaring, who didn't sympathize with any of your struggles at all, be they personal or job-related? Have you ever ordered food at a fast-food restaurant and thought, *Well, I don't know why this person taking my order works here. She obviously doesn't want to be here and is not enjoying her job at all.*

Even these kinds of scenarios can help us gain experience in life and benefit us as far as the kinds of attitudes we carry. These attitudes teach us the way we should *NOT* be. Having been a teacher, I made it a point to go the extra mile and to show that I did indeed care for my students. One reason is that I had a teacher once like the one I described above. I have supervised people and have always tried to do so in a positive and interested manner. I have never taken food orders at a fast-food restaurant, but my job as a minister involves showing an interest in the people I serve, and I sincerely attempt to do that. My mother Shirley used to tell my twin brother Bill when he was a boy, "Attitude!--Attitude!"

She wanted him to adjust his. Who would have thought he would become a pastor one day? For that matter, I am sure I surprised a few people too when I became one!

In Matthew 20:28, we read, "Just as the Son of Man did not come to be served, but to serve, and to give his life as a ransom for many." Jesus, the Son of God, came to this earth and made Himself a servant in order to meet people's needs. He was still the Deity, but He came to minister to people's needs. When we take a servant's approach as a teacher, a supervisor, a customer service employee, or whatever the case may be, we will find treasures in the darkness, and the people we work with will appreciate our example. Maybe this is not the kind of comment that blesses everyone, but a few people over the years have said to me, "You are a kind person." To me, that is one compliment I am pleased with and believe is important.

Determined Devin

I recently viewed a DVD documentary about a remarkable man named Devin Dearth. This champion bodybuilder, who was in great shape, suffered a stroke at the age of forty. He barely survived and lost much of his ability to speak or even move. Yet this man was determined. He went through all of the physical therapy with a passion which doctors and nurses said they had never seen before. He was sent home because the insurance company refused to allow the therapy to continue. Learning of a hospital in China that used acupuncture and various methods to stimulate the nerves and hearing about a woman's remarkable recovery who was a patient there, Devin was convinced he needed to go to China. His church helped raise the necessary money, and he was on his way.

It wasn't always easy, but after just one day, he could raise his right leg, which he had previously been unable to do. He worked hard and made progress, gaining more movement and speaking more clearly. His son graduated from high school while Devin was in China. There were sacrifices made. He didn't see his wife at times who occasionally had to return home for their children's sake, but his wife Stacey stood by his side and supported him.

At one touching part in the documentary, a therapist was teaching Devin to clearly say, "I love you, Stacey," to his wife, and his eyes welled up with tears. He knew his wife had been a treasure in his darkness. She helped frequently with the therapy and did not allow this tragedy to change her love for her husband.

Devin, with two family members at each side, walked into his home church when he returned to the United States. Everyone stood and cheered for him. Here was a man who had learned to find treasures in darkness. Devin's family, including his brothers, stood with him without hesitation. The documentary featured a scene of one brother going to the gym with Devin. The DVD ended by telling the viewer that Devin planned to return to China for more therapy.

The Dearth family's story is filled with examples of treasures being retrieved from the darkness. What treasure can you retrieve from your dark places today? Does the treasure include a family member who stood with you during a difficult time? Does the treasure include making progress toward one of your goals although you have not reached it yet? Does the treasure include a group of friends or a church doing something extraordinary for you? What treasure can you pull from the darkness today?

Is there a Song in Your Heart?

Chippy the parrot didn't see it coming. His owner had decided to clean Chippy's cage, but as she was finishing her vacuuming, the phone rang. She picked up the receiver and accidently sucked Chippy up into the vacuum. She felt terrible and immediately grasped poor Chippy from the clutches of the vacuum cleaner. She hosed Chippy down with water and then used her hair dryer on him to dry him off. She placed him back in his cage.

The same friend who had called, inadvertently causing the accident, called a few weeks later to check on Chippy. "Chippy doesn't sing much anymore," reported his owner. "He just sits and stares."

Have you ever felt that way? You have been sucked up into a vacuum called life, and you have been through a whirlwind experience. Life has hosed you down and dried you off with intense heat, and now the song has gone out of you, and the wind has left your sails. You no longer sing a song of joy. You just sit and stare and can't figure out what happened.

You have heard the term "regroup." Sometimes, we need a small break in order to reflect on what went wrong. Then we need to resolve to move ahead with a positive attitude. We must determine that our hearts will not be silent. We will still sing a song in our hearts. Our dream will not shrivel up and die. But we will believe that this setback was really a set-up for a comeback! As the lyrics joyfully tell us in "The Color of Roses," a song by Beth Nielsen Chapman, "Only the ones who believe ever dream what they see, ever dream what comes true" (Lyrics by Beth Nielsen Chapman). Believe! Sing! Chippy was meant to sing, and you were meant to believe in your dreams.

Psalms 105 verse 2 says, "Sing unto him, sing psalms unto him: talk ye of all his wondrous works." Keep singing those hymns and choruses, even when circumstances are not the best. Even Job said that God gave him a song in the night (Job 35:10).

Believe in the Darkness

The word "believe" is a powerful word. We must believe our dreams are possible, or all of our efforts will be in vain. Tara Lipinski, who won Olympic gold in 1998 in Nagano, Japan, skated to that song during her tour with "Stars on Ice."

On February 21, 2002, Sarah Hughes skated the performance of her life in Salt Lake City, Utah, and captured the Olympic gold medal. She catapulted from fourth place in the short program to first place in the long program and in the final standings. She said, "I just went out to skate and to have fun and had a great time" (NBC TV interview). She enjoyed the moment, and she seized the moment. We must remember to enjoy the journey as we travel toward our goals.

Sarah as a young child stated her goal was to get to the Olympics and to win a gold medal. She said, "I can't wait for that to happen" (NBC TV video). Sure, she was just a child, but she also drew a picture of herself on the top podium at the Olympics when she was attending elementary school. She had faith that it would one day happen. It did.

The Treasures of Darkness

To repeat Beth Nielsen Chapman's words again: "Only the ones who believe ever dream what they see, ever dream what comes true."

We read in St. Mark 9:23, "Jesus said unto him, if thou canst believe, all things are possible to him that believeth."

Coincidence or Christ?

Is it a coincidence or Christ? In life, sometimes hard-to-explain situations occur, but they are only difficult to explain if we try to explain them outside of the Lord. For example, my grandparents Henry and Emma Fornash raised me from the time I was three months old. I always tell people that they were just like Grandpa and Grandma Walton from the old TV series. He was always laughing and cutting up, and she was sweet with a touch of vinegar.

I will always be grateful to them that they raised me in church and demonstrated God's love in front of me. They were unashamedly affectionate to me and to each other. They seldom quarreled, but when they did, they soon forgave each other. They did not hold grudges. They were hard-working people who raised a garden every year in their retirement years. My grandmother canned peaches, corn, pickled beans, and other fruit and vegetables.

As my grandfather moved up in years, I prayed that God would not take him until I was at least eighteen years old. In my mind, I could handle it better because I would be legally an adult. My grandfather passed away on February 10, 1978, just months before I graduated from high school. He was just shy of his eighty-sixth birthday, which would have been on March 27. Guess how old I was? I was eighteen years old, just as I had asked the Lord to let me be at the time of his death.

The "coincidences" do not end there. My dear grandmother passed away twenty-one years later. The date? It was February 10, 1999, the same date (the tenth of February) that my grandfather had passed away. It seemed appropriate since they loved each other so much. They practically worshipped each other. And since they both passed away on this date, I think I accepted my grandmother's death a little easier, believing that it was God's appointed time.

I am not yet done. The day before, on February 9, 1999, I had visited my grandmother in the care center where, thankfully, she spent just a very short time. She had broken her hip a few months before and needed constant care. She was now ninety-six years old, and I knew her time was very near to go to her eternal reward. As I prepared to leave, I did not know it would be the last time I would see her alive, but I said, "I will see you in the morning." She passed away that night.

I later thought that it was appropriate I said, "I will see you in the morning," because there is a hymn that says, "I will see you in the morning just inside the eastern gate over there" (The Eastern Gate, Isaiah G. Martin, 1905).

I later wrote an article about the reunion that I believe will take place someday, and I wrote that I will see my grandmother in heaven again. It was published by a religious magazine, and I mentioned that my last words to her had been, "I will see you in the morning." I sent the article out in the spring of 2002. It was published on February 9, 2003, exactly four years to the date after I had said, "I will see you in the morning." I had no control over the publication date. That was

God! That was the Lord! That was not a coincidence, but that was Christ! Don't misunderstand me—I do not believe that every little thing means something special. But it still amazes me to this day that I was thirty-three years old and my grandmother was ninety-one years old when she came to live with me in her last years, and the last four numbers of the telephone number given to me when we moved into a house together was "3391."

I don't need to dwell on that to believe that God was in our lives while we were together, and that He is still in mine. His Word tells me that in the latter part of verse 20 of Matthew chapter 28, "lo, I am with you always, even unto the end of the world."

Jesus's disciple Peter denied three times that he knew the Lord after Jesus had warned him he would do this. Peter went out afterward and wept bitterly (John 18:27, Matt. 26:75). Yet after Jesus's resurrection, He restored Peter, and, interestingly enough, had Peter confess Him in front of other people three times, the same amount of times Peter had denied the Lord (John 21:15-17).

Even little things can mean a lot, such as a date of February 10. God reveals Himself to us if we are paying attention. Are you paying attention? Watch for the little things. Is it a coincidence, or is it Christ?

Praying in the Shower

There is a great scripture about the favor of God found in Psalms 5:12. It says, "For surely, O Lord, you bless the righteous; you surround them with your favor with a shield" (NIV).

I believe we can pray for the favor of God. I have prayed for it for myself and my family and friends. Recently, my brother, also a minister as well as a pastor, gained permission from a county sheriff to visit a relative in jail. Usually this is not allowed. When he arrived for the visit, the attendant didn't believe he could visit his own relative, and she was not going to allow him in. He told her to check with the sheriff, and after a quick phone call, she motioned to him and said, "You can go in now, Rev. Carpenter."

Obviously, he had gained the favor of the sheriff. God knows how to place us in the right place at the correct time so that we may gain favor. Joseph gained favor with Potiphar, and eventually he gained favor with the most powerful ruler on the earth at the time, Egypt's pharaoh. He was made the prime minister of Egypt, second in power only to Pharaoh himself. Joseph had been placed in a pit at the start of his unusual journey, placed there by his jealous brothers who were jealous of their father Jacob's favoritism towards Joseph. So, Joseph went from the pit to prison (falsely accused by Potiphar's wife) to the palace of Pharaoh!

Do you need God's favor, especially today? Let me encourage you that God is only a prayer away. When I began a new job as a writer for reviews of films for The Dove Foundation in December 2005, I was starting just before the Christmas break, and their offices would be closed for the entire week. I was a new employee, and I would not be paid during this time. I imagine Christmas is a costly time for most families. I remember praying in the shower for God to meet my family's needs. My wife told me she overheard me praying in the shower before she rose from the bed that morning. At our Dove Christmas party for employees just before the Christmas break, my supervisor handed me an envelope and told me that the board of directors had decided to give me a bonus. I was blessed to learn that the contents of the envelope included an entire week's pay for the Christmas week when the offices would be closed! I was so grateful, and I knew God's favour was with me. Now, my wife wants me to pray in the shower all the time!

It Worked Out Just Fine

Romans 8:28 tells us that all things work together for good for those who love God and for those who are called according to His purpose. Certainly you can think of something which happened to you in the past which didn't start off very well but it had a nice ending. Maybe you didn't like a certain job for the first few days, but then you began to get to know your fellow employees and the job itself. As you gained knowledge on the job, your confidence grew, and, suddenly, you liked the job!

Billy Graham was in love with a girl early in his ministry, but things did not work out. He was heartbroken. Yet he continued serving the Lord. A short time later, he met a young woman named Ruth who was the daughter of missionaries. Eventually they married, and over fifty years later, she was still his companion. He said she had greatly helped him over the years and influenced his life and ministry in positive ways. Yet he met her after an earlier romance did not pan out. This is another example of things working out in the long run.

When you enter into a new venture or a new territory, don't be too quick to judge or decide you don't like it. It could be that things are going to work out just fine.

Keep Praying!
God uses Unlikely People

The Bible tells us in St. John 15:7 that if we abide in Christ and His word abides in us, we can ask what we will and it will done for us. Years ago when I was helping a pastor out in a small church, a young woman named Penny asked for prayer. Her husband had left her to raise three kids by herself. She was working as a waitress at a restaurant, doing the best she could. Then, her car broke down. She was finding it difficult to simply get back and forth to work. So, we prayed for her. A week later, she brought us a great report. She told her boss about the situation, and he had a used car that he didn't need. He *gave* the car to her! I will never forget her next comment. "You don't know my boss," she said. "He doesn't do things like that!" Yet his generosity was well-timed and an answer to prayer. Penny made us laugh when she added, "It's not a Rolls Royce, but it rolls! That's all I care about!"

During your times of walking in the secret places of darkness, God will send some encouragement along. Just remember, you may be going through a time of testing and trials, but that does not mean that God ceases answering prayer. Keep praying!

Mercy

In Psalms 136, 1-9 and in other verses in that same chapter, we read that the Lord's mercy endures forever. The Bible also tells us that His mercies are new every morning (Lamentations 3: 21-23) just as the sunrise brings us a new day. One of the treasures of darkness in this life is the knowledge that things truly could be worse and God is working behind the scenes on our behalf.

Adam and Eve were driven out of the Garden of Eden after the fall, and cherubim, angelic-like creatures, were placed there to guard against their return. There was a flaming sword which turned each way to forbid entrance. God wasn't being cruel. He had a better plan than man living forever in a state of sin, with its painful consequences. He promised in Genesis chapter 3 that the seed of women, Jesus, who was born of the Virgin Mary, would one day bruise the head of the serpent (Satan). God promises in Romans 6:23 that although the wages of sin is death, the gift of God is eternal life through Jesus Christ our Lord. His mercy is certainly revealed in this scripture.

He also made Adam and Eve coats of skins since they were naked, which enables us to realize that God Himself made the first animal sacrifice with the shedding of blood in order to clothe His creation. Again, His mercy was revealed.

Cain, the offspring of Adam and Eve, killed his younger brother Abel, and yet God showed mercy to him too. Even though God declared that Cain would be a vagabond in the earth for his wicked deed, He set a mark on Cain so that others would not take vengeance upon him. This was due to the fact that Cain cried out for mercy, and the Lord's mercy endures forever.

In St. Mark 10:46, Bartimaeus, the son of Timaeus, was blind, and when he heard that Jesus was walking the dusty road of Jericho, he cried out to Jesus to show mercy upon him. The disciples tried to quiet Bartimaeus, but he cried out the louder. Jesus called him to Him, and Bartimaeus asked Jesus to restore his sight. Jesus did, and Bartimaeus saw the One who had performed this miracle.

St. Matthew 5:7 says that if we show mercy to others, God will show mercy to us. Let us show mercy to others and store up mercy for we will need it someday. David showed mercy to Saul, even after Saul chased after him to kill him due to his jealousy as he knew David would be the next king of Israel. When David needed mercy after committing adultery and having his baby die, God showed him mercy and forgave his sin. One of the treasures of darkness is looking to God in hope for His mercy, which is new every morning and endures forever.

Running on Empty?

I once heard a humorous story about a little girl who had a stomachache, and she complained to her mother. "Your stomach hurts, dear, because you have nothing in it. You haven't eaten yet today. You need something in it, and you will feel better." Later that evening, the family had the pastor over for dinner. At one point, the little girl's mother asked, "Pastor, are you feeling okay?"

"I have a headache," replied the pastor.

"That's because there's nothing in it!" said the little girl. "If you put something in it, you will feel better."

We may smile at this story, but it makes a good point. We need to be filled with God's Word and His Spirit, and we need to nourish our souls with uplifting thoughts. It helps to hang around upbeat people too. When we are discouraged, it's because, in some cases, we have emptied of the good things which keep us upbeat. Acts 1:8 says we shall have power after the Holy Spirit has come upon us. Jesus never left anyone empty. He filled the stomachs of the multitude with plenty of bread and fish. The Bible tells us that he filled barren wombs. God gave Hannah a baby after she prayed for one, and Mary's cousin Elizabeth had a child in her older years.

Remember to keep yourself filled with good things so you won't feel empty. God gives us good treasures when, even during difficulties, we are filled with good things and have the right frame of mind.

Be Encouraged! God is Faithful!

Look for the light when you are in darkness! Some months ago, I filled in for several Sundays at a church in Whitehall, Michigan, which had been without a pastor for a short time. When I arrived to fill in that first Sunday morning, I could tell the people were terribly disappointed in their pastor that had just resigned. I could sense they hadn't seen it coming. Some of them were frustrated, and a few were a bit angry. Some people had left the church. God gave me a message that morning from 1 Corinthians 10:13 about God being faithful, and I could tell the timing was right. It encouraged the people. I told them I knew God had already prepared the next pastor for the church, and he would soon be on the way. Only a few months later, I filled in for the last time. They actually had requested a resume from me, but I knew in my heart I was meant to encourage them, not shepherd them. Sure enough, they found a pastor they were very excited about. In just a few months, I saw this congregation go from being discouraged to being excited. My simple message on "God is faithful" may be an illness or financial difficulties or the resignation of someone you cared about from your job or church. Rest assured--God is faithful. Look for the light! God will not leave you hanging!

Noble Goals

In Luke 1:37, we read, "For with God nothing shall be impossible." In order for us to bring forth treasures from dark places, we must never let regrets take the place of our dreams. It is so very important for us to realize our dreams, or a void will always linger in our souls.

Joni Erickson Tada didn't allow an accident which paralyzed her to halt her dreams. She has written books and painted, and she has been a speaker on radio and television. She also found happiness when she married some years ago. Not only are these awesome accomplishments, but to achieve these things while spending a lot of time in a wheelchair should inspire all able-bodied people to work hard to accomplish their dreams.

Think of it this way—if years ago a dictator such as Adolf Hitler could write a book titled *Mein Kampf* with all of its hatred and prejudices, then those with lofty goals of writing good books or songs should be able to reach their own noble goals with a little elbow grease and perseverance. If your goal is something else, the same principle applies. Don't live with regrets. Live with accomplished goals. God said that with Him, all things are possible.

Temper! Temper! Temper!

The book of James says in chapter 1 verse 19 that we should be slow to anger. I once preached a message titled "Temper! Temper! Temper!" Have you ever noticed if you take the letter "d" from the beginning of the word "danger," you are left with the word "anger"? And when we become angry, we walk on thin ice and are in danger. A person who will find treasures out of darkness is the person who will move past moments of anger. A man who battled his temper quite often once commented to his pastor, "I only shoot off my temper quickly, and then it's over."

"That's kind of like a shotgun," replied the pastor. "It only takes a moment too, but it shoots everything to pieces." The point is well-made. Our temper has repercussions.

I once was driving the highest speed of the speed limit on a freeway, and a driver passed me on the left on the *SHOULDER* of the road, like I was driving twenty-five miles per hour. I could have gotten angry, but instead I just shook my head and prayed for the person's wisdom to grow. I won't say I have never had a few moments of anger on the road, but I have learned the hard way that a temper let loose can be worse than a cannon which has gone off.

If you have ever observed anger in someone else, you are aware that it can be an ugly trait. The Bible tells us in Titus 1:7 that a bishop, or leader in a church, must not have a quick temper. This is because this spiritual person is supposed to be an example of how we should live. Someone said if you ever intend to give someone a piece of your mind, make sure you can get by on what's left!

The Bible tells us to be slow to anger (Ps. 103:8). In Ephesians 4:6, we are instructed not to go to bed angry at someone. I once heard of a husband and wife who had an argument. The husband had heart problems, and shortly after the disagreement, he died of a heart attack. Can you imagine the grief and guilt the wife must have felt? It is important that, as much as we can, we live in peace with others. When we do, we will find some treasures in the darkness, treasures which come from forgiveness and self-control.

Seed Planter

2 Corinthians 9:6 says, "But this I say, he which soweth sparingly shall reap also sparingly, and he which soweth bountifully shall reap also bountifully."

In order for good treasures to come into our lives, we must plant seeds during the difficult times when we are not bearing fruit. The fruit will eventually come forth after we plant the seeds.

It's not necessarily a lot of joy for farmers to till their land in the spring and to plant and water and work hard when there is nothing to show for it in the beginning.

In Proverbs 20:4, the Bible says a lazy man will not plow when he should, and when harvest time comes, he has nothing to show for it.

Have you been sowing into your dreams? If you have musical abilities, have you been practicing regularly? If you are called to preach, do you study, and are you prepared? If you are planning a trip you want to take, are you keeping the vision before yourself and working out your travel plans by faith?

I recently heard Joel Osteen say that there are many people in graves today who did not write the books they should have written or lived the dreams they should have lived because they put it off. The book of James, chapter 4 and verse 14, tells us that life is like a vapor, such as one sees on the bathroom mirror following a shower. It is there for a moment and then gone. It is like a foggy wooded area which you see on a morning commute, but a short while later, the fog has lifted. Life moves quickly, and then it's over. What will you leave behind? Are you planting seeds?

Keep Moving Forward

To quote Rocky Balboa from the film *Rocky Balboa (MGM,2006)*, "Life isn't about how hard you can hit but about how hard you can get hit and keep moving forward." Heb. 11:1 speaks about faith as the "evidence of things not seen." Isn't that the way we should live? We should live like our situation is going to be okay, even when it doesn't look like it. To experience the treasures of darkness, one must be willing to get up when one is knocked down. Any heavyweight champ who ever held the title for at least a few years experienced getting knocked down and then getting back to his feet.

The Bible says that a just man shall fall seven times, but he keeps getting back up (Prov. 24:16). Life can knock us down by a hurtful comment from a friend or someone we know or by denying us the promotion we wanted or by a bad medical report or by a variety of other ways. Yet those who experience the spoils of victory or hold a championship belt in their hands are those who were knocked down but found the strength to get back up one more time.

To use Rocky Balboa again as an illustration, in the film *Rocky II*, Rocky knocks the champ Apollo Creed down in the fifteenth round, but the punch carries his own tired body to the canvas. Now, they both attempt to get up before the count of time. Rocky has been knocked down. He is tired. He is beat up. But somehow, as the referee's count hits ten, Rocky climbs to his feet to barely beat Apollo Creed, who sits on the canvas, unable to rise. Rocky is the new heavyweight champion of the world! Yet he didn't win because he was a more skilled fighter, but it was "will over skill." He got up before the bell rang.

A few minutes later, holding the championship in his hand, Rocky thanks God and then says to his wife Adrian, who is watching by the TV, "Yo, Adrian, I did it" (*Rocky 2, United Artists, 1979)!* He holds the belt, the symbol of victory, above his head. Adrian had believed in him, and he came through. We too can win at life if when we get knocked down, we get up one more time. A wise man said, "You win at life by getting up once more than you were knocked down."

More than One Way to Receive an Answer to Prayer

The other day, a friend of mine who has lost one leg and gets around in a wheelchair told me of his frustration after purchasing an electronic bus ticket worth $40 so the man who helps take care of him could get around on the bus to run errands. An error was made by the transit company, and when the man went to use the ticket, it came up empty, meaning the mistake that was made cost my friend Will $40 because it was never added to the electronic ticket.

I told Will about the time that some people owed me $35 for a job, and they ignored it and didn't pay me. I prayed about it instead of showing a temper, and within a few days, a lady in our church sent my wife Jackie and me a $35 check, saying she "felt led" to do it. She did not know that the $35 was the *exact* amount that we had been cheated out of. I prayed for Will that God would restore his $40. I told him God could restore that $40, just as He had restored our $35. Within several days, he called me, all excited to tell me the following story.

He had to buy a new part for his handicapped bathroom in his home, and he wasn't sure of the cost. Just before he bought it, a friend from church brought the part to him at church one day, saying he wanted to take care of it for him. When Will looked at the box, the price of the part was on the box. Guess how much it cost? That's right, $40 exactly! God restored that money to Will. Will received the part he needed, and he didn't have to spend a dime.

One of the ways we experience the treasures in the dark times is by keeping our peepers open so that we see how God restores to us what has been stolen away by the enemy of our faith. The Bible says in Mark 11:23, "Have faith in God."

Confess the Ugly

I happen to enjoy watching old silent films of the great actor Lon Chaney. Chaney was raised by deaf parents and learned early on to be expressive with his face and mannerisms. He was the perfect actor for the silent film era.

In probably his most famous film *The Phantom of the Opera,* he is unmasked by an innocent woman he has fallen in love with named Christine. When she pulls off his mask, she reveals a hideous face. The Phantom is at first angry and then moved to tears as he covers his face in his hands because Christine has exposed his ugliness. Christine is shocked by his visage.

There are ugly things in all of us from time to time. We may try to mask them, but they are there, be it jealousy, envy, deceit, etc. The way to bring treasures out of the darkness is to do what the book of James says to do and confess our faults one to another (James 5:16). It means shortcomings. Only Jesus needs to hear the sin and really bad stuff, although one may feel at ease with a relative or friend enough to share some of the ugliness beneath the surface.

When we remember we are human and make mistakes, it may also remind us to have mercy on others when a nasty temper or some other ugliness is revealed.

Your Gift

I recently preached about the future from Revelation chapter 3 and how the Christian has a lot to look forward to. I believe Christ will receive His own, and the holy city, New Jerusalem, will come down from God out of heaven; and God will be with His people, and His people will serve Him and live in the paradise which God had originally planned for man in the garden of Eden.

After this particular service, one of our church members, a middle-aged man named Dale, told me he could see a lot of passion and excitement in me as I preached the message. I replied to Dale that I have never felt such a sense of fulfillment as when I preach the gospel. I know it is because I am doing what I am called to do and supposed to do. I am in my element. It may not be a large talent, but God has given me a gift to communicate.

It doesn't mean we don't have challenges in our callings and when we use our talents. Everyone has a tough day at work. Even LeAnn Rimes, the famous country singer, once had a bad outing on a talent search TV show before she hit the big time. There have been a few times when I have stumbled over my words, or the people who listened to me didn't respond as much as at other times.

Your Gift

At times, the sermons I preach come easily, and at other times, I feel as if I am banging my head against the wall to get a timely topic.

The point is, if we continue to use our gifts and talents even when we struggle, we will have those moments in which we shine. We will find some wonderful moments of treasures from the dark places. When God gives us a gift, He enables us to use it.

Eyes on the Only Perfect Man to Ever Live

Tiger Woods's extra-marital affair is in the news everywhere as I write. Only a few weeks ago, I used to think, *When it comes to sports, the media sure makes a hero out of Tiger Woods.* Don't misunderstand. I recognize he is a very gifted athlete, and from what I have read, a very disciplined one who has studied his craft for years on end. Yet I have noticed that whenever a person is placed on the proverbial "pedestal," he or she inevitably falls. I add quickly that I'm sure Mr. Woods never asked to be placed up there on that vaunted pedestal. Yet the media loved him, and his fall has been a real "thud" in the sporting world.

The Bible tells us in Hebrews 12:3 to "fix our eyes on Jesus..." He is one who was tempted as we are when He walked this earth, but He never had a failure. He was tempted like we are yet found without sin.

Several years back, I placed a pastor on a pedestal, and inevitably, he "fell" on me! He let me down, and I learned he was indeed, after all, human. There is nothing wrong with appreciating people and their accomplishments, but we should never place anyone on a pedestal. I don't want anyone placing me on one (fat chance they would!). When we learn that people are simply human and frail and everyone has weaknesses, then instead of placing them on a pedestal, we will help them up when they fall. That is another treasure we can bring forth from the darkness.

Slow but Worth the Wait

*S**low.* Sometimes things happen much slower than we would like. I once read about a man who was sitting in his living room one day when he heard a very light tap at his door. He answered it and saw no one but then noticed a snail at his feet. Without saying a word, he picked it up and threw it across the street. Two years later, there was a light tap at his door again. He opened it up, and there at his feet was the snail. "What was that for?" asked the snail. I smile every time I read or hear that story. It seems as if we wait that long, two years and more, to sometimes just get back to where we were financially or in our goals or for things to begin to come together.

The Bible tells us in Ecclesiastes 3:11 that God makes everything beautiful in its time. It can take a while to paint a portrait or to make a work of art or to write a great novel or to get to where we want to be. God uses time for our advantage, although we sometimes grow impatient. Waiting on God will teach us that He brings treasures out of darkness.

God Uses Imperfect People

The Bible says in Romans 11:29, "For the gifts and calling of God are without repentance" (NIV). In today's modern English, we would say that God does not change His mind about the gifts He has given. If you have a gift of communication, such as to teach or preach, God has given you that gift, and He will not change His mind. If you have a gift of administration, there may be times you won't receive the opportunity to use it for a bit, but God will not take the gift away from you. He does not take back gifts, such as the talent to sing, to write, or to create. He does not take back ministry gifts. The greatest challenge we face sometimes is in losing the confidence we should display in God and in ourselves. He wants us to use our gifts with confidence.

Some time ago, I came across an anonymous piece in a newsletter. This piece makes it clear that one doesn't have to be perfect to be eligible to be used by God. In fact, isn't there a beauty in the cracked Liberty Bell? It is unique, and we don't mind the imperfection. Neither do we mind the imperfection in the Leaning Tower of Pisa. There are reminders that nothing is perfect; nevertheless, imperfect things and people can still be useful to God and to mankind. Here is the anonymous piece:

> The next time you feel like God cannot use you, remember the following people: Noah was a drunk, Isaac was a day dreamer, Leah was ugly! Moses couldn't speak well, Samson had long hair, Timothy was too young, Elijah was suicidal, Jonah ran from God, Job went bankrupt, Peter denied Christ, Martha worried about everything, Zaccheus was too small, Paul was too religious, Abraham was too old, Jacob was a liar, Joseph was abused, Gideon was afraid, Rahab was a prostitute, David had an affair and was a murderer, Isaiah preached naked (thank God we no longer have THAT tradition!), Naomi was a widow, John the Baptist ate bugs, The disciples fell asleep while praying, Mary Magdalene was demon possessed, the Samaritan woman was divorced, more than once
>
> Zaccheus was too small, Paul was too religious, Timothy had an ulcer...AND Lazarus was dead (Daily Focus, Jim Daly's Blog)!

Faith with Works is Active Faith

I heard about a minister who wanted to travel from church to church to preach and spread the good news of God's love to man. He believed this was a calling and what he was meant to do. Yet some time passed, and the minister received no offers or open doors. He decided to take a step of faith. He took a trip to the local department store and bought some luggage, just to show he had faith that he would soon be traveling. Right after this, he received an opportunity, and soon his calendar filled up.

The Bible states in James 2:17, "Even so faith, if it hath not works, is dead, being alone" (KJV). So then faith without works is dead, just as the body without the spirit is dead. A person who works fifty hours a week will make more money than the person who does the same job at the same place but works forty hours. How much have you put into the sack? Whatever you put in the sack is what you will get in return.

I once had a financial need, and so I put some scripture promises in my wallet, such as Philippians 4:19, which states that God shall supply all of my needs. In a short time, my finances improved. I believe it was because I put some action into practice to show I had faith. Maybe you are in a situation right now where some action is called for as evidence of your faith. If you have not seen anyone commit to Christ recently, tell someone about God's love! Be like the college student who when he moved into his dorm, placed a large "V" over the door. Someone asked him if it stood for "victory." He replied, "No," but he would make no further statements. Four years later, when he graduated as the class valedictorian, it was evident what the "V" had stood for. He set the goal before him and by faith saw himself achieving it. You too will bring forth treasures out of darkness if you put your faith into action by works.

Evidence

The Bible says in Matthew 7:20, "Wherefore by their fruits ye shall know them" (KJV). The fruit which we bear tells those around us just what kind of people we are. If you manage to keep a sense of humor during difficult times, it tells people you know how to get through life. If you are patient with your children, people realize there is a maturity inside you as a parent and that you are a caring parent. The fruit we bear can speak to our own selves if we pay attention. If we are irritable, then either something is bothering us or we aren't getting sleep! If we speak in bitterness and anger, there are unresolved issues inside us.

The famous detective Sherlock Holmes, created by Sir Arthur Conan Doyle and played brilliantly in the Granada TV series by the late Jeremy Brett, gathered together the "fruits" of a case, or the evidence, and then built his case. If he caught someone in a lie or found evidence left behind at the scene of the crime, he began to weave his case. He built his case on these pieces of evidence.

The fruit we bear are pieces of evidence in revealing where we are in life. Are we happy? Are we miserable? Are we generous? Are we stingy? Do we think of others? Do we think only of ourselves? Are we unthankful? Are we grateful?

Someone once said that if you went to trial and were being prosecuted for being a Christian, would there be enough evidence to convict you? What kind of fruit have you been bringing forth? It will tell you where you are. The way to find treasures in darkness is to starve the dark side of ourselves that tries to take over and to feed that good side. Trusting in God's Word and promises helps us to bring forth good fruit.

The Summary

How do I summarize this journey? The definition for summary is: a brief statement or account of the main points of something. And I will indeed be brief. From scriptures and my life experience I have endeavored to show that by trusting in the Lord during difficult times that things can work out for the best in the long run, and that we can gain valuable knowledge and experience. You may feel as if the shade has been pulled on the brightness in your life at times, but God is able to and indeed does raise that same shade when morning comes. He offers hope. Psalms 30:5 says, "For his anger endureth but a moment; in his favour is life: weeping may endure for a night, but joy cometh in the morning." (KJV).

As previously quoted, Romans 8:28 offers us a vast hope even when we walk the dark hallways of life. "And we know that all things work together for good to them that love God, to them who are the called according to his purpose." (KJV)

I say, along with the Lord Jesus Christ, "It is finished." (John 19:30). Jesus meant he had accomplished the plan of salvation, he had completed the task that God the Father had entrusted him with. He had trusted the Father and the Father trusted him. I thank the

Lord for enabling me and giving me the strength to finish this task. It has been over a period of many years. The manuscript was even lost once for a few years. But he helped me and gave me grace. It is finished.

CPSIA information can be obtained
at www.ICGtesting.com
Printed in the USA
LVHW012157181119
637710LV00026B/1086